W9-AYP-313

A Pocket Guide to Writing in History

A Pocket Guide to Writing in History

Second Edition

Mary Lynn Rampolla
Trinity College

Bedford/St. Martin's   Boston   New York

For Bedford/St. Martin's

History Editor: Katherine E. Kurzman
Developmental Editor: Charisse Kiino
Production Editor: Bridget Leahy
Marketing Manager: Charles Cavaliere
Copyeditor: Barbara G. Flanagan
Text Design: Claire Seng-Niemoeller
Cover Design: Hannus Design Associates
Composition: Karla Grinnell Goethe
Printing and Binding: Haddon Craftsmen, Inc.

President and Publisher: Charles H. Christensen
Editorial Director: Joan E. Feinberg
Director of Editing, Design, and Production: Marcia Cohen
Managing Editor: Elizabeth M. Schaaf

Manufactured in the United States of America.

2   1   0   9   8
f   e   d   c   b   a

For information, write: Bedford/St. Martin's, 75 Arlington Street, Boston, MA 02116 (617–426–7440)

ISBN: 0–312–18006–3

Preface

For many students, the paper assigned in their first-year history survey is also their introduction to writing a college-level essay, a situation that they — and their instructors — may find less than satisfactory. Though many students understand that college papers must do more than restate information gleaned from lectures and books, they may have only a vague idea of how to go about researching, writing, and documenting a history paper. Instructors, for their part, must convey a great deal of information about history and historical methodology in a limited amount of time, often in large lecture classes; thus, they can rarely devote more than one or two periods to writing instruction. *A Pocket Guide to Writing in History* was designed with just such situations in mind. The response to the original version of this manual, which was conceived as a supplement to Diana Hacker's *A Pocket Style Manual*, was a pleasant surprise: pleasant, because it was very enthusiastic, and a surprise, because most instructors were using *A Pocket Guide to Writing in History* as an independent text, not in conjunction with *A Pocket Style Manual*, as we had anticipated. One of the major changes in this revised edition, therefore, is that it is designed to stand alone; cross-references to *A Pocket Style Manual* have been eliminated, and supplemental material has been added on some grammatical issues of special concern to historians.

Like the original edition, this manual introduces students to the conventions of writing in history, provides an overview of typical assignments, and offers advice on research and using sources. It also includes abundant documentation models based on *The Chicago Manual of Style*. This new edition also incorporates revisions suggested by users of the first edition: the discussion of plagiarism has been significantly expanded; using, evaluating, and citing Internet sources is discussed in several places; and new sections have been added on writing essay exams and making outlines. Like the first edition, *A Pocket Guide to Writing in History* is brief and accessible and can be tucked into a pocket or bookbag.

While preparing this manuscript I benefited from the advice and encouragement of my colleagues and students at

Trinity College in Washington, D.C. I am especially indebted to the following historians for their thoughtful reviews of the first edition: René De La Pedraja, Canisius College; Greg Kaster, Gustavus Adolphus College; Michael L. Krenn, University of Miami; Cathy Kudlick, University of California, Davis; Robert M. Levine, University of Miami; Robert G. Mangrum, Howard Payne University; Justin D. Murphy, Howard Payne University; Peggy Anne Phillips, University of Miami; John Robinson, Front Range Community College; Barry T. Ryan, Point Loma Nazarene College; and John M. Vander Lippe, SUNY College at New Paltz.

At Bedford Books, I would like to thank Chuck Christensen and Joan Feinberg, who conceived the idea for this manual and supported the idea of a revised and expanded edition. I would also like to thank my editor, Charisse Kiino, for her excellent insights and suggestions at every phase of this project; Elizabeth Schaaf, the managing editor; Katherine Kurzman, the sponsoring editor; and Barbara Flanagan, who copyedited my prose with precision and care.

Finally, I would like to thank Barbara Fister of Gustavus Adolphus College, who compiled the detailed, up-to-date list of research sources that concludes this manual.

Mary Lynn Rampolla
Trinity College
Washington, D.C.

Contents

Introduction:
How Historians Work

On the old television police series *Dragnet,* Sergeant Friday curbed the speculations of his witnesses with a stern admonition: "Just the facts, Ma'am. Just the facts." Students who take their first college history class with a sense of foreboding often think that historians, like Joe Friday, are interested only in compiling lists of names, dates, places, and "important" events that happened sometime in the past. But history is much more than that. Historians are not interested just in what happened and when, although such facts are important to them. They also want to know why events happened and how those events are related. Historians evaluate, organize, and interpret a wide variety of facts, derived from a wide variety of sources, in an effort to understand the world of the past.

History is a complex discipline and historians are a diverse group. They take different approaches to their material; they interpret the events of the past in different ways; they even disagree on such basic issues as whether and to what extent historians can be objective. Regardless of their approaches, however, historians see writing as an important tool of inquiry and communication.

In addition to introducing you to some of the basic elements of what historians do, this manual provides guidelines for writing papers in the field of history. Of course, the vast majority of students enrolled in their first history course are not contemplating a career in history; indeed, most history majors follow career paths that lead them away from the study of the past into fields like law and government, business, and international relations. Nevertheless, the techniques you will need to master to write an effective history paper — how to read critically, think analytically, argue persuasively, and write clearly — are skills that will be useful to you wherever your academic interests take you and that you will value in whatever career path you choose to follow.

Historical questions

Historians come to their work with a deep curiosity about the past; to satisfy that curiosity, they ask questions. It has been suggested that historians are like detectives; it is certainly true that they ask some of the same questions as detectives, like Who? What? When? Where? and Why? Some of these questions are designed to elicit "the facts" and are relatively easy to answer: Who was the emperor of Japan during World War II? What tools did eighteenth-century weavers use? When did the Vietnamese drive the Khmer Rouge out of Phnom Penh? Where did the first Continental Congress meet? Other questions, however, are less easy to answer: Who was Jack the Ripper? What were the religious beliefs of the peasants of twelfth-century Languedoc? When did President Nixon learn about the Watergate break-in? Where did the inhabitants of the original settlement at Roanoke go, and why did they disappear? More complex questions such as these have formed the basis of absorbing historical studies.

Historians also ask questions that help them analyze relationships between historical facts. Many of the questions historians ask, for example, reflect their interest in understanding the *context* in which the events of the past occurred. For example, a historian interested in the scientific revolution of the seventeenth century would not simply write about scientific "advances," such as Copernicus's theory that the sun, and not the earth, was the center of the solar system. Rather, the historian would also ask questions about historical context: What role did political issues play in the acceptance or rejection of Copernicus's theory? Why did some theologians find his ideas threatening to religion, while others did not? What impact did larger social, political, and intellectual movements, like Renaissance humanism or the Reformation, have on the study of astronomy in this period? In other words, historians do not examine events in isolation; rather, they try to understand the people and events of the past in terms of the unique historical context that helped to shape them.

As they explore the relationships between and among events in the past, historians also ask about the *causes* of events. The historical events that you will be studying and writing about can almost never be traced to a single cause, and historians are careful to avoid simplistic cause-and-effect relationships as explanations for events. For example, although the assassination of Archduke Franz Ferdinand was the event that precipitated World War I, no historian would argue that it *caused* the war. Rather, historians try to uncover the complex multiplicity of causes that grow out of the historical context in which events occurred.

Historians also ask questions about the relationship between continuity (events, conditions, ideas, and so on that remain the same over time) and change. Many of the questions historians ask reflect this interest. For example, a historian who asks "What impact did the Black Death have on the economic and legal status of the peasants?" is interested in examining the changes brought about by the bubonic plague against the backdrop of the ongoing institution of serfdom.

Finally, while the past doesn't change, historians' interests — and the questions they ask — do. Historians, like the people they study, are part of a larger context; they are guided in their choice of subject and in their questions by their own interests and by the interests and concerns of their societies. As they ask new questions, historians look at sources in new ways. They may even discover "new" sources — sources that had always existed, but had been ignored or dismissed as irrelevant. History, therefore, is a vital and dynamic discipline; we will never know all there is to know about the past because we are constantly posing new questions, and our questions, in turn, help us to see the past in new ways.

The best way to enter the world of the historian is to ask as many questions as you can about the particular historical issues you are studying. As you seek the answers to your questions, be aware of the new and more complex questions that your answers raise and let them guide your exploration further.

Historical sources

To answer their questions, historians examine and evaluate a wide variety of sources. These sources fall into two broad categories: *primary sources* and *secondary sources.* To study history and write history papers, you will need to know how to work with both kinds of sources.

Primary sources

Primary sources are materials produced by people or groups directly involved in the event or topic under consideration, either as participants or as witnesses. Examples of primary sources include eyewitness accounts, decrees, letters and diaries, newspapers and magazines, speeches, autobiographies, and treatises. Tax rolls, census data, and marriage, birth, and death registers can also be primary sources. In addition, historians sometimes examine primary sources that are not written at all, like coins, works of art, films, recordings, or archaeological remains. For recent history, oral sources, such as interviews with World War II veterans or Holocaust survivors, can also be primary sources. By examining primary sources, historians gain insights into the thoughts, behaviors, and experiences of the people of the past.

When using a written primary source, it is important to *read the source itself.* Do not simply rely on another historian's analysis of the source; the purpose of writing history, after all, is to develop *your own* interpretation based on the evidence you have assembled. If possible, you should read the whole source, rather than excerpts from a reader. When you are writing a history paper, you need to know the *significance* of the entire document and the *context* of any portions of the source that you wish to discuss or quote. Moreover, in the process of choosing excerpts, an editor is making a judgment about what aspects of the source are important; in effect, he or she is determining the significance of the source for you. However, sources can yield different kinds of information depending on the questions the historian asks; therefore, it is preferable to read primary sources in their entirety.

Secondary sources

Historians also use *secondary sources:* books and articles in scholarly journals that comment on and interpret primary sources. Secondary sources are extremely useful. Reading secondary sources is often the simplest and quickest way to become informed about what is already known about the subject you are studying. In addition, reading scholarly books and articles will inform you about the ways in which other historians have understood and interpreted events. Finally, secondary sources can be an important research tool. Reading them carefully can help you find a subject for a research paper by pointing you toward topics that have not yet been explored fully or about which there is controversy. Moreover, the bibliographies of secondary sources can direct you to primary sources. As valuable as they are, however, you should never base a history paper entirely on secondary sources. Whenever possible, you should study the events of the past in the words of people who experienced, witnessed, or participated in them.

Primary or secondary?

The status of a source as primary or secondary depends on the question you ask. If you are writing about the reign of Richard III (1483–85), your primary sources might include edicts, chronicles composed by contemporary witnesses to the events of his reign, and letters written by foreign ambassadors to the English court. Strictly speaking, Thomas More's *History of Richard III,* written in the early sixteenth century, would be a secondary source because More was not a witness to the events he describes, and he records only the evidence provided to him by others. If, however, you are writing about the depiction of Richard III in the early Tudor period, More would be a primary source.

Evaluating sources

If sources always told the truth, the historian's job would be much easier – and also rather boring. But sources, like witnesses in a murder case, often lie. Sometimes they lie on purpose, telling untruths to further a specific ideological, philosophical, or political agenda. Sometimes they lie by omission, leaving out bits of information that are crucial to interpreting an event. Sometimes sources may mislead unintentionally; the author was not aware of all the facts, or misinterpreted the facts, or was misinformed. Many are biased, either consciously or unconsciously, and contain unstated assumptions; all reflect the interests and concerns of their authors. In any case, historians' sources often conflict; two different sources may tell two very different stories. As a result, one of the challenges you will face in writing a history paper is evaluating the reliability and usefulness of your sources.

One way in which historians evaluate primary sources is to compare them; a fact or description contained in one source is more likely to be accepted as trustworthy if other sources support or corroborate it. Another technique historians use to evaluate the reliability of a source is to identify the author's biases; we might be less inclined, for example, to believe Polydore Vergil's assertion that Richard III killed his nephews if we realize that he was the official court historian for Henry VII, who killed Richard in battle and seized the throne for himself. Historians also read their sources very carefully for evidence of internal contradictions or logical inconsistencies, and they pay attention to their sources' use of language, since the adjectives and metaphors an author uses can point to hidden biases and unspoken assumptions.

Secondary sources may also contradict each other. Several historians can examine the same set of materials and interpret them in very different ways. Similarly, historians can try to answer the same questions by looking at different kinds of evidence or by using different methods to gather, evaluate, and interpret evidence. You can use the same techniques to evaluate a secondary source as you would use to evaluate a primary source: compare your source with other secondary sources; identify biases and unconscious assumptions; and look for logical inconsistencies. Most important, however, you should return wherever possible to the primary sources and consider whether the author uses and interprets the sources appropriately. The study of the ways in which historians have interpreted the past is called *historiography,* and knowing how to read and evaluate the work of other historians is so important that some professors may ask you to write a historiographic essay (see pp. 17–18). In any case, to get the most out of your reading of secondary sources, you will need to study a variety of interpretations of historical events and issues and learn how to read carefully and critically. (For a fuller discussion, see pp. 7–10, "Reading Critically.")

How this manual can help you

When you do research and writing in a history course, you will become a participant in historical debate. As you devise questions about historical topics and seek answers in primary and secondary sources, you will begin to come to conclusions about those topics. In the papers you write for your history courses you will construct arguments about those conclusions and offer support for them. This manual will help you understand the process from start to finish. After introducing typical assignments in history, the manual describes conventions of writing that are specific to the discipline. It then discusses how to use sources effectively. Finally, it explains how to give proper credit to those sources.

History, like the other arts and sciences, provides a window onto the ideas and beliefs, the actions and passions, of human beings. Reading and writing history entail above all an exploration of who and what we are. This manual is designed to aid you in such exploration and to help you discover the pleasures of studying history.

Approaching Typical Assignments in History

The reading and writing projects assigned to you in a history course will give you opportunities not only to learn more about historical issues, events, and people but also to act as a historian by contributing your own ideas to the field. This section begins with a discussion of critical reading; reading is, after all, the assignment you will encounter most frequently in your history courses. This is followed by a review of the most common types of short writing assignments you might encounter — ranging from summaries, book reviews, and annotated bibliographies to short papers and historiographic essays — with suggestions for some general ways of approaching these assignments. The section ends with a discussion of essay exams.

NOTE: Many professors include detailed instructions with their writing assignments. You should always read these instructions carefully, follow them closely, and ask for further explanation if you do not fully understand them. The suggestions here are meant to complement your professor's guidelines, not in any way to replace them.

Reading critically

History courses typically require a great deal of reading from a wide variety of sources. If your professor has assigned a textbook, you will probably be expected to read a chapter or two each week. You may also be asked to read a variety of secondary sources, including articles from scholarly journals or books about a particular aspect of your topic. Many professors also assign primary sources, documents ranging from medieval chronicles to legal documents to newspaper accounts. (For a fuller discussion of the types of documents historians use, see pp. 3–6). Furthermore, if you are writing a research paper, you will need to find, read, and analyze a variety of sources pertaining to your topic that are not part of the reading assigned to the whole class.

Since reading is such an important assignment, it is essential to give serious consideration to *how* you read. Reading for a history course is not like reading a novel; it is not enough to skim each page once and get the gist of the story. In fact, as you do your reading assignments, you must accomplish several tasks: you need not only to understand the content of what you are reading but also to analyze its significance, evaluate its usefulness, and synthesize all of your reading into one coherent picture of the topic you are studying. Careful and critical reading is crucial both for active and intelligent participation in class discussion and for writing effective papers.

The best way to become a careful and critical reader is to become an *active* reader, constantly asking questions of the texts you are reading. Following are some questions you should ask of the sources you read.

WHAT CAN THIS SOURCE TELL ME? What does the title tell you about what the source covers? What purpose does the author lay out in the introduction? If the source is a book, what topics are presented in the table of contents?

IS THE SOURCE PRIMARY OR SECONDARY? Both primary and secondary sources can provide valuable information; however, they provide different kinds of information. If you are studying nineteenth-century communes, for example, primary sources such as the diaries or letters of commune members can provide firsthand information about the thoughts, feelings, and daily lives of the people who lived in them. Primary sources would be less useful, however, in helping you understand the larger, sociological effects of communal living. To get a better understanding of those effects, you might turn to secondary sources in which historians offer a broader perspective on communes, perhaps examining several such communities over time. (See pp. 3–6 for a fuller discussion of primary and secondary sources.)

WHEN WAS THE SOURCE PUBLISHED? If it is important that you know the most recent theories about a historical subject, you should pay special attention to the publication dates of the sources you are considering. A 1996 article reviewing theories about construction of Native American burial mounds may contain more recent ideas than a 1964 review. You should not assume, however, that newer interpretations are always better; some older works have contributed significantly to the field and may offer interpretations that are still influential. (As you become more experienced in historical research, you will be able to determine which older sources are still useful.) Moreover, older sources might offer a historical perspective on how interpretations of an issue or event have changed over time.

CAN I TRUST THIS INTERNET SOURCE? Of course, this is an important question to ask of any source, but Internet sources present special problems. The most significant difficulty that students encounter when trying to evaluate an Internet source is that, while articles in scholarly journals and books from academic presses are carefully reviewed by other scholars in the field, anyone with the right software can post information on the Internet. (One student found a medieval "chronicle" on the Internet and quoted it extensively in her paper; unfortunately, it turned out to be completely fictitious.) Students should therefore be especially careful to determine the reliability of their Internet sources: Is the author affiliated with a college or university? Is the article's Web site affiliated with an academic institution, press, or journal? If you are unsure of your source, it is best to consult your professor or a reference librarian.

DOES THE AUTHOR PROVIDE SUFFICIENT AND LOGICAL SUPPORT FOR HIS OR HER THESIS? Any book or article makes an argument in support of a thesis. Once you have identified the thesis, you should evaluate the evidence the author uses to support it. You may not be in a position to judge the accuracy of the evidence, although you will build expertise as you continue to read about the subject. You can, however, evaluate the way in which the author uses the evidence he or she presents. You might ask yourself whether the evidence logically supports the author's point. For example, the eighteenth-century French philosophe Denis Diderot advocated religious tolerance, but this fact does not justify an assertion that all eighteenth-century Frenchmen were tolerant. Such an assertion would be a logical fallacy known as a *hasty generalization*.

You should also ask whether the same facts could be interpreted in another way to support a different thesis. For example, G. Stanley Hall, a prominent American psychologist of the early twentieth century, amassed evidence that demonstrated a correlation between a woman's educational level and the number of children she had: women who attended colleges and universities had fewer children than their less-educated sisters. From these facts, he concluded that higher education caused sterility in women. A modern historian looking at the same evidence might conclude that education allowed women to become economically independent, freed them from the necessity of forming early marriages, and allowed them to pursue careers other than raising children.

Another consideration is whether the cause-and-effect relationships described in a source are legitimate. It may be true that event A happened before event B, but that does not necessarily mean that A caused B. For example, an extremely bright comet was visible all over Europe in the autumn of 1066. That winter, Duke William of Normandy conquered England. We should not necessarily assume, however, that the comet caused the Norman conquest. This would be a *post hoc* fallacy, from the Latin *post hoc, ergo propter hoc* ("after this, therefore because of this").

In addition, you should consider how the author deals with any counterevidence. (See pp. 35–36 for a discussion of counterevidence.)

WHAT IS THE AUTHOR'S VIEWPOINT AND BACKGROUND? Authors write from particular points of view that are determined by many factors, including their personalities, interests, and experiences. Introductions and prefaces can help you determine how an author has approached the subject and alert you to background that might have influenced his or her positions or interpretations. For example, in the Autobiographical Postscript to his edition of *Gilgamesh,* Herbert Mason reveals that he was profoundly affected by the death of his father, an event that influenced his interpretation of the epic poem.

HOW DOES THE SOURCE COMPARE WITH OTHERS I HAVE CONSULTED? Does the source add to your knowledge of the subject? How is it different from other sources you have read? Does the author contradict or disagree with others who have written on the subject? If so, which arguments or interpretations do you find most convincing?

Writing history papers

Aside from research papers, which will be discussed in a separate section, the most common writing assignments you will encounter are summaries, book reviews, annotated bibliographies, short essays, and historiographic essays. Each requires a slightly different approach.

Summaries

Your professor might ask you to summarize a document, an article, or a section of a book. Because summarizing requires you to condense what you have read and put the author's ideas *into your own words,* it helps ensure that you have understood and digested the material. A summary (sometimes called a *précis*) should describe the author's main point, or thesis, and key evidence used to support it. A summary, then, essentially reports the content of the text; it should not include your critical analysis of the text. (See pp. 23–24 for further advice on writing summaries.)

Book reviews

A book review is not the same thing as a book report, which simply summarizes the content of a book. When writing a book review, you not only report on the content of the book but also assess its strengths and weaknesses. Students sometimes feel unqualified to write a book review; after all, the author of the book is a professional historian. However, even if you cannot write from the same level of experience and knowledge as the author, you *can* write an effective review if you understand what the assignment requires.

In writing a review you do not just relate whether or not you liked the book; you also tell your readers *why* you liked or disliked it. It is not enough to say, "This book is interesting"; you need to explain *why* it is interesting. Similarly, it is not enough to report that you disliked a book; you must explain your reaction. Did you find the book unconvincing because the author did not supply enough evidence to support his or her assertions? Or did you disagree with the book's underlying assumptions?

To understand your own reaction to the book, you need to read it carefully and critically.

As a critical reader, you are not passive; you should ask questions of the book and note reactions as you read. Your book review then discusses those questions and reactions. (See pp. 7–10 for advice on critical reading.) Though there is no "correct" way to structure a review, the following is one possible approach.

- Summarize the book and relate the author's main point, or thesis. (Somewhere early in the paper, identify the author briefly.)
- Describe the author's viewpoint and purpose for writing; note any aspects of the author's background that are important for understanding the book.
- Note the most important evidence the author presents to support his or her thesis.

- Evaluate the author's use of evidence, and describe how he or she deals with counterevidence. (See pp. 35–36 for a discussion of counterevidence.) Is the book's argument convincing?
- Compare this book with other books or articles you have read on the same subject.
- Conclude with a final evaluation of the book. You might discuss who would find this book useful and why.

NOTE: *Critical* does not mean negative. If a book is well written and presents an original thesis supported by convincing evidence, say so. A good book review does not have to be negative; it does have to be fair and analytical.

Annotated bibliographies

A bibliography is a listing of books on a particular topic, usually arranged alphabetically by authors' last names. (See pp. 48 and 63–71 for further information on bibliographies.) In addition to providing bibliographic information, an annotated bibliography briefly summarizes each book or article and assesses its value for the topic under discussion. In writing your entries for an annotated bibliography, keep in mind the same questions you would ask while writing a book review. Remember that entries in an annotated bibliography should be relatively short; you will not be able to write a full analysis of a book or article.

Following is an example of an annotated bibliography entry:

Duus, Peter, ed. *The Japanese Discovery of America: A Brief History with Documents.* Boston: Bedford Books, 1997.

This book explores the relationship between Japan and the United States in the mid-nineteenth century, focusing on the dramatic differences between the two cultures and the uneasiness, confusion, and misunderstandings that arose from those differences. In a short introductory history, Duus discusses Japanese isolationism; the military and economic factors that led the United States to forcefully open relations with Japan; and the ways in which the Japanese observed and interpreted Americans and their culture. The main body of the text comprises a series of documents, including political pamphlets, autobiographies, eyewitness accounts, broadsheets, and prints. The inclusion of both Japanese and American views of Japan invites a comparison of mutual misunderstandings.

History papers: General approaches

History students are most often asked to write two types of papers: short essays and research papers. Although these papers are different in some respects, they require similar approaches.

Primary sources are of central importance to historians. (See p. 3.) Nevertheless, historians do not simply take the evidence provided by such sources at face value. Like good detectives, they evaluate the evidence. For example, in a letter written to Sheik El-Messiri in 1798, Napoleon expresses the hope that the sheik will soon establish a government in Egypt based on the principles of the Qu'ran, the sacred text of Islam. Those principles, according to Napoleon,[1] "alone are true and capable of bringing happiness to men." Should we assume, on the evidence of this letter, that Napoleon believed in Islam? A historian might ask, "Do we have any other evidence for Napoleon's attitude toward Islam?" "What do other primary sources tell us about Napoleon's attitude toward religions such as Catholicism, Protestantism, and Judaism?" "Do any other primary sources contradict the attitude toward Islam expressed in Napoleon's letter to the sheik?" In other words, "How accurately and to what extent can this source answer questions about Napoleon's religious beliefs?" In addition, historians try to understand or interpret their sources even if those sources do not offer the best or most accurate information on a certain topic. As it happens, Napoleon did not believe in Islam. This does not mean, however, that his letter to the sheik should be relegated to the dustbin. Instead, a good historian will ask, "Under what circumstances did Napoleon write this letter?" "Who was Sheik El-Messiri, and what was his relationship to Napoleon?" "What does this letter tell us about Napoleon's willingness to use religion to his political advantage?" To write about historical questions, you will need to know how to approach many different kinds of primary sources and ask appropriate questions of them.

History papers usually include a narrative that recounts "what happened." Narrative is a basic element of history writing, and it is crucial that your account of past events is accurate. Nevertheless, a series of factual statements about

---

1. Napoleon Bonaparte, "Letter to the Sheik El-Messiri" in *The Mind of Napoleon: A Selection from His Written and Spoken Words,* 4th ed., trans. and ed. J. Christopher Herold (New York: Columbia University Press, 1969), 104.

the past, however precise they may be, does not constitute a history paper. You will not have written a history paper if you report that something (for example, the Manchu invasion of China, the death of the Aztec king Montezuma, the rise of Islam) happened. Rather, a history paper explores *how* and *why* something happened and explains its significance. In essence, when you write a paper in history, you are expected to interpret sources and, using those interpretations, to come to a conclusion about the meaning and significance of your subject. You express this conclusion in the main point, or thesis, of your paper. To support your thesis, you offer evidence and respond to counterevidence, information that seems to contradict or weaken your thesis. (See pp. 29–32 for a discussion of the thesis and pp. 35–36 for a discussion of counterevidence.)

Remember that professional historians, working from the same sources, often form very different opinions about them. Thus it is unlikely that there is one "correct" interpretation of any topic that you will write about. You do, however, need to convince readers that your interpretation is a valid one. You will be able to do this only if you have provided *concrete evidence* that supports your thesis and have responded honestly to opposing positions.

Short essays

Unlike most research papers, essays are relatively brief (about five to ten pages), and the topic and text(s) are usually assigned. You might be asked, for example, to analyze a source or group of sources and respond to a specific question about them. Here is an example of a short essay assignment for a class in the history of science:

> Compare the views expressed by Nicole Oresme [a late-medieval natural philosopher] and Galileo Galilei on the role of religious beliefs in the study of the natural world.

In a different class, you might be asked to write an in-depth analysis of one text or to compare the views of two modern historians on the same issue. However different these assignments may appear to be, they all require similar responses.

ANALYZE THE ASSIGNMENT CAREFULLY. What will you need to know in order to write this paper? Make sure you identify and understand *all* the parts of the assignment. For the history of science example, it would not be sufficient to write a paper about Galileo using a few references to Oresme for comparison; you would need to understand what *both* Oresme and Galileo think about the role of religious beliefs in the study of the natural world and give approximately equal weight to each in your discussion. Because the assignment asks you to compare the views of Oresme and Galileo, you would also need to understand both how their views are similar and how they differ.

You should also be careful to write about the topic that has actually been assigned. In reading Oresme and Galileo, for example, you may discover that both discuss the extent to which a natural philosopher should rely on the authority of Aristotle. Although this is an interesting issue, it is not the subject of the assignment.

CONSIDER THE SIGNIFICANCE OF THE MATERIAL. It is not enough to present a "laundry list" of similarities and differences or to report the contents of the texts you have read. Nor should your paper be composed of two "mini-papers" — one on Oresme and one on Galileo — glued together. Instead, when you write a history paper, you are expected to consider the significance of the issue you are examining. In the sample assignment, the instructor's expectation is that the student will examine not only the ways the two authors are similar and different but the meaning of those similarities and differences. In responding to the sample assignment, you might discover, for example, that both Oresme and Galileo believe in God as the creator of the universe and the author of the natural laws that govern it. In writing the essay, you would be expected to discuss why this similarity is important. Or a comparison of the two texts might reveal that Oresme believes that the Bible can answer questions about the natural world, while Galileo argues that Scripture has no place in scientific discussions. In that case you should discuss the significance of this difference.

You should also think about the historical issue underlying the assignment. In this essay assignment, the student is asked to compare the views of Oresme, a fourteenth-century natural philosopher, with those of Galileo, who, two centuries after Oresme, became a central figure in the scientific revolution. One purpose of this assignment might be to encourage the student to think about the relationship between medieval and early modern views of the world.

CONSTRUCT AN ARGUMENT IN SUPPORT OF A THESIS. A short essay, like any paper in history, should have a thesis that is supported by evidence presented in the body of the essay. Your thesis reflects what you have concluded about the issue after careful reflection on the assignment and any reading that you have done for it. (See pp. 29–32 for further discussion of the thesis.) The student who concludes that Oresme's and Galileo's ideas are similar would write a thesis about the significance of those similarities:

> Popular descriptons of Galileo imply that he believed science and religion to be incompatible, but a comparison of his ideas with those of Nicole Oresme suggests that Galileo's ideas about God and nature were very similar to the beliefs held by medieval natural philosophers.

The student who concludes that the differences between Oresme and Galileo are more significant than their similarities would write a thesis reflecting such an interpretation:

> Both Galileo and Oresme believe in God, but the similarity ends there; while Oresme sees Scripture as the ultimate font of all knowledge, Galileo dismisses it as irrelevant to the issues explored by scientists.

Note that the writers of these two theses have read the same texts and arrived at opposite conclusions, neither of which is "right" or "wrong." What is essential is that the students be able to support their theses with evidence taken from the texts. It is not enough simply to make an assertion and expect readers to agree.

RESPOND TO COUNTEREVIDENCE. Acknowledging counterevidence — information that does not support your argument — will *not* weaken your paper. On the contrary, if you address counterevidence effectively, you strengthen your argument by showing why it is legitimate despite information that seems to contradict it. If, for example, you wish to argue for continuity between medieval and Renaissance science, you would need to show that the similarities between Galileo's and Oresme's ideas are more significant than the differences. If you want to argue in support of the differences between the two, you might try to show that their similarities are superficial and that Galileo's rejection of Scripture as a source of knowledge about the natural world constitutes a significant change in the way people thought about science. In either case, your argument must be based on evidence and counterevidence contained in the relevant texts, not merely on your own "gut feelings." (See pp. 35–36 for further discussion of counterevidence.)

DOCUMENT YOUR PAPER. Even a short essay requires that you cite and document the sources of your information. (See pp. 44–47 for a discussion of when to cite sources. Models for how to document various kinds of historical sources can be found beginning on p. 50.)

Historiographic essays

Historians frequently disagree about how to interpret the events they study. For example, some historians have interpreted the Magna Carta, a charter signed by King John of England in 1215, as a revolutionary declaration of fundamental individual freedoms; others have seen it as a conservative restatement of feudal privilege. Similarly, historians interested in the same historical event might examine different sets of sources to answer the same question. In studying the causes of the French Revolution, Marxist historians might focus on economic and class issues while intellectual historians might concentrate on the impact of the writings of the philosophes (a group of French Enlightenment writers) on political thought and practice. To make students aware of debates among scholars and to acquaint them with a variety of interpretations, some instructors ask their students to write historiographic essays.

A historiographic essay is one in which you, acting as a historian, study the work of other historians. When you write a historiographic essay, you identify, compare, and evaluate the viewpoints of two or more historians writing on the same subject. Such an essay can take several forms. You might be asked, for example, to study the work of historians who lived during or near the time in which a particular event happened—for example, to explore the ways in which contemporary Chinese historians wrote about the Boxer Rebellion. A different kind of historiographic essay might require that you look at the ways in which historians have treated the same topic over time; for example, to examine how historians have treated Richard III, you might begin with the account of Sir Thomas More and end with the most recent study of Richard's reign. A different kind of historiographic essay would ask you to compare the views of historians from several historical "schools" on the same event. You might, for

example, be asked to compare Whig and Progressive interpretations of the American Revolution or Marxist and feminist
views of the French Revolution. But in any case, a historiographic essay focuses attention not on a historical event
itself, but rather on how historians have interpreted that
event.

A historiographic essay combines some of the features
of a book review with those of a short essay. You should
begin by reading critically the texts containing historians'
interpretations, keeping in mind the questions you would
need to answer if you were going to write book reviews
about them (see p. 10). You should not, however, treat the
historiographic essay as two or three book reviews glued
together. Rather, you should synthesize your material and
construct an argument in support of a thesis. Following is a
thesis from a student's essay on historians' interpretation of
the colonial period of African history:

> Historians have held dramatically different views about the
> importance of European colonial rule in Africa: Marxist his-
> torians, along with others who focus on economic issues,
> have tended to see the colonial period as an important
> turning point, while cultural historians have maintained
> that the impact of the West on the ancient cultural tradi-
> tions of Africa was superficial.

In the rest of the paper, the student supports the thesis, using
the guidelines set out for a short essay (see pp. 14–16).

Revising and editing your paper

One of the biggest mistakes that students make with any
writing assignment is to leave themselves too little time to
revise and edit their work. Although some students take a
rather perverse pride in their ability to write a passable
paper the night before it is due, the resulting work is never of
the highest caliber and usually bears the hallmarks of care-
less writing: sloppy mistakes in reasoning, awkward constructions, poor word choice, and lack of clear organization,
not to mention spelling and grammar mistakes. To write an
effective history paper, you must allow yourself time to revise
your paper.

When you revise, you need to read your paper critically,
as if it were someone else's work. (For advice on critical
reading, see pp. 7–10.) You should read for logic and clarity.
You should make sure that your evidence is sufficient and
that it supports your thesis. You should also look for wordi-
ness and awkward sentence structure, for repetition and

cliché. You must be willing to rearrange the order of material, do additional research to support weak points in your argument, and even change your entire thesis, if necessary. Obviously, you need to allow plenty of time for this part of the writing process, which may involve several drafts of the paper.

NOTE: Running the spell checker and grammar checker on your computer *is not* the same as revising your paper. Moreover, running the spell checker will not pick up incorrectly used homophones (for example, *their, there,* and *they're*). Nor should you rely on your grammar checker to catch every mistake. Always edit and proofread the final copy of your paper carefully; your instructor will not look kindly on a paper that is full of typographical, grammar, and spelling errors.

Taking essay exams

The essays you write for an exam will necessarily be shorter than the papers you write for your course, but they should follow the same basic format. In other words, an exam essay should begin with a thesis, stated clearly in the first paragraph, followed by several paragraphs in which you provide evidence supporting your thesis, and end with a conclusion. The difficulty, of course, is that you will be writing *this* essay under pressure, in a limited period of time, and without the opportunity to check the accuracy of your data.

Here are some suggestions for preparing to write a successful essay on a history exam.

Preparing for the exam

The best preparation for an exam does not begin the day, or even the week, before the exam but takes place throughout the semester. Careful reading of the texts and periodic review of your notes on a weekly basis will ensure that you have a firm grasp of the material come exam time.

Throughout the semester, you should do the following.

- Attend class regularly and take good notes. It is not necessary, of course, to write down *everything* your professor says. When taking notes, you should listen for the professor's *main points* and note the evidence that he or she gives to support those points. (You will discover that your professor's lectures usually follow the same format as a good essay.) Follow the same suggestions for a discussion class; your classmates will often make important points about the material you are studying.

- Review your notes regularly, preferably after each class. If you review your notes while the class is fresh in your mind, it will be easier for you to notice places where the notes are unclear. Mark these places and clarify confusing points as soon as possible, either by researching the issue yourself or by asking your professor.

- Refer to your syllabus throughout the semester. Many professors provide detailed syllabi that state the themes for each section of the course. Use this as a guide for your own studying and thinking about the course material.

- Take careful notes on the material you are reading for the course. Keep in mind that simply copying long sections from your texts is not very useful in ensuring that you have understood the material. It will be much more useful for you to take notes in the form of summaries (see pp. 10–11 for a fuller discussion).

- If one is not assigned for the course, consider keeping an academic journal. In your journal, record important points about the material you are reading, any questions you want to answer or issues you would like to raise, important ideas suggested by class discussions, and so on. You can use the journal to track your growing knowledge of the material you are studying.

The week before the exam

- Review your notes, syllabi, and texts. Identify the most important themes and issues of the course and assemble the evidence that elucidates those themes.

- Imagine that you are the professor faced with the task of setting the exam for this course. What questions would you ask? Framing your own exam questions and answering them can be a useful way of organizing your thoughts.

Taking the exam

BEFORE YOU WRITE. *Do not begin to write right away.* This is probably the biggest mistake that students make in essay exams. Before you write, do the following.

- Read the exam carefully. Make sure you understand what each question is really asking. You will not gain points by scribbling down everything you know about the development of Chinese politics from the tenth through the fifteenth century when the question asks you to discuss the impact of the Mongol invasion in 1260.

- If you are offered a choice, make sure you answer the question you can answer best. This may not always be the one you are drawn to first. One great insight about the significance of the Treaty of Waitangi will not be enough to write a good essay about Maori-British relations in nineteenth-century New Zealand. Be sure that you can cite several pieces of evidence in support of your thesis.
- Take the time to organize your thoughts. Jot down a quick outline for your essay, stating the thesis and listing the evidence you will provide to support that thesis.

WRITING THE ESSAY. Once you are ready to write, your essay should follow the same format as any other history essay.

- Begin by stating your thesis. *Do not* waste time restating the question — your professor knows what he or she asked.
- Cite the evidence that supports your thesis. If you are aware of any counterevidence, make sure you discuss it. (See pp. 35–36 for a discussion of counterevidence and how to deal with it.)
- Be sure you *stick to the point*. Do not go off on interesting tangents that are irrelevant to the question. Referring frequently to your outline will help you keep on track.
- Tie your essay together by stating your conclusions.

Writing a Research Paper

A research paper, like a short essay, usually takes the form of an argument with a thesis supported by evidence. It is different from a short essay, however, in several ways. A research paper is more substantial, usually at least fifteen pages and often much longer. More important, a research paper, as its name implies, requires that you supplement required read-ings for the course with information from the library and other sources.

Your instructor might assign a specific research topic, or the choice might be left entirely up to you. Most often, you will be given some choice within a general area. The syllabus for a course with a research paper might, for example, include a statement like this in its list of course require-ments:

> Research paper on any topic covered in the course, chosen in consultation with me. Your paper should be 15–18 pages and is worth 40% of the final grade.

Students often find such assignments intimidating and may secretly yearn for an assigned subject; it often seems easier to write about a topic that holds no interest for you than to face the task of defining your own area of investigation. However, when you choose your own research topic, you are engaged in the practice of history at a much more sophisti-cated level. You are, in fact, doing the same work that a pro-fessional historian does: answering the questions *you your-self* have posed about a subject that you find compelling or problematic.

Following is some advice to consider before you begin a research project.

Thinking about your topic

A research paper represents a significant investment of time and effort. Before you begin, therefore, you should think very carefully not only about your interests but also about the fea-sibility of your proposed topic.

CHOOSE A TOPIC THAT INTERESTS YOU. Start with the texts assigned for your class and find a general area that appeals to you. To begin with, your subject can be relatively broad, for example, "slavery and the Civil War"; you will not know what problems, issues, and questions exist within the larger framework of the broad topic until you familiarize yourself with the general subject.

In deciding on a topic, you should also think about what sources are available to you. For example, you might decide that it would be interesting to examine the views of artisans during the French Revolution, but if you cannot obtain enough sources of information on this subject, or if they are available only in a language you cannot read, this will not be a workable topic.

START YOUR RESEARCH EARLY. The day you receive the assignment is not too soon to begin your research. Anticipate problems in gathering your sources: other people may have borrowed the books you need, or you may have to travel to other libraries to use their collections. If you are interested in a topic for which your own library has only limited sources, you might be able to borrow books from other colleges and universities on interlibrary loan. But to ensure that you get your books in time, you will need to make your request early.

Taking effective research notes

Your final paper will be only as good as the notes you take. There is no right or wrong way to take notes for a research paper. Many people favor 4" x 6" or 5" x 8" index cards, which can be arranged and rearranged easily. Others prefer to use notebooks or legal pads. If you have a laptop computer, you may wish to type your notes directly into an electronic file. This can be especially useful if you use a word processing program with a global search function so that you can use the search command to find key words quickly wherever they appear in your notes. But whatever method you use, there are several things you can do to make your note taking more effective.

ALWAYS RECORD COMPLETE BIBLIOGRAPHIC INFORMATION FOR ANY SOURCE YOU CONSULT. Nothing is more frustrating than to return all your books to the library, only to discover that you are missing authors' names, dates of publication, or other information you will need for your bibliography. (See p. 63 for a description of the elements that constitute "complete bibliographic information." If you have not written many academic papers, you may find it difficult to remember all of these elements; therefore, while doing your research, you may want to keep this guide handy. Or you may find it useful to list the information you need to record on an index card that you can carry with you.)

TAKE MOST OF YOUR NOTES IN THE FORM OF SUMMARIES. If you take notes word for word from your source, you are simply acting as a human photocopier. Your goal should be to digest the information presented in your sources and make it your own. It is therefore much more useful to read carefully and thoughtfully, close the book, and summarize in your own words the section you have read. Then compare your summary with the original, noting any important points that you missed or anything that you misunderstood. This type of note taking not only will ensure that you really understand the material but also will help you avoid plagiarism.

NOTE: Even if you are summarizing, you must note the source of your information and cite the source in your paper. Students sometimes assume, erroneously, that they need to document only direct quotations. In fact, "borrowing" ideas from other writers without documenting them is a form of plagiarism every bit as serious as stealing other writers' words. Any time that you use information derived from another person's work, adopt someone else's interpretation, or build on another writer's ideas, you must acknowledge your source. (See pp. 44–47 for a fuller discussion of avoiding plagiarism.)

AVOID THE MISCONCEPTION THAT "TO PHOTOCOPY IS TO KNOW." Photocopying material on your topic is no substitute for reading and understanding it. Photocopying doesn't save time; in fact, it's often a time waster. Eventually, you will have to read and interpret the photocopied material, and when you do, you may notice that you have copied irrelevant material and missed important information.

COPY QUOTATIONS ACCURATELY. If you do decide to quote directly from a source, make sure you copy the words and punctuation of your source exactly; do not try to improve the wording of the original or correct the spelling or grammar. You may, however, alert your readers to an error in spelling or grammar by recording the error as it appears in the source and then noting the mistake by adding the Latin word *sic* in brackets, as follows: "Do not correct mispelled [*sic*] words."

Getting ready to write

A great deal of the work you do in writing a research paper happens *before* you begin to write your first draft. Following are some important steps that precede the drafting stage.

USE BOTH PRIMARY AND SECONDARY SOURCES. In a research paper, you will need to consult primary sources (letters, diaries, original documents, and so on) from the period you are studying. You will also want to consult secondary sources to become familiar with the ways in which other historians have interpreted this material. Do not confine your research to books; important recent research is often found in articles in scholarly journals. (See Appendix B for guidance in researching primary and secondary sources.) Your instructor will be able to direct you to additional sources. Librarians are also extremely helpful in tracking down both printed and Internet materials.

USE BOTH PRINT AND INTERNET SOURCES. The Internet has had a profound impact on the ways in which students do research; through the Internet, students in even the smallest colleges in the most isolated settings can have access to a wide variety of historical materials. However, it is important to remember that many primary and secondary sources are not yet available on the Internet. Students who rely solely on electronic media will inevitably miss many fundamental and indispensable sources. It is vital, therefore, that you consult both electronic and print sources in your research.

GENERATE A WORKING BIBLIOGRAPHY. The first step in finding a topic for your research paper is to generate a working bibliography. You should begin your search in the library. If your professor has suggested sources, make sure you consult them at the outset of your research. Invaluable and often overlooked resources are reference librarians, who can direct you to important journals, bibliographies, and other research tools. Reference librarians can also teach you how to conduct an online search by using key words to find recent books and journal articles in your library's collection. If your library has a card catalog, be sure to check it as well; many college libraries are still in the process of computerizing their holdings, and you may overlook important sources if you rely solely on the computer. You may also be able to use your library's computer to search the holdings of nearby affiliated libraries; and, of course, you can conduct an Internet search as well.

Once you have found some preliminary sources, you can use their notes and bibliographies as a guide for gathering additional material.

NOTE: Do not make generating a bibliography an end in itself — you still need to read the books and articles you have found. Your final bibliography should include only the materials you have read and found useful in writing your paper.

NARROW YOUR SUBJECT DOWN TO A WORKABLE TOPIC. Once you have begun to gather materials related to your area of interest, you will need to narrow your subject down to a workable topic. After all, you will not be able to write effectively on a broad topic like "slavery and the Civil War" within the length of a typical research paper.

Narrowing your topic to one that is feasible always begins with reading; however, simply reading everything you can find about slavery and the Civil War will *not* help you find a suitable research topic. Your reading must be active, not passive. In other words, you must be actively engaged in a dialogue with the texts you are reading, constantly asking questions that direct your reading.

A history paper usually begins with a question, and you can begin to narrow your broad subject by rephrasing your topic as a series of questions. What is it that you want to know about "slavery and the Civil War"? Are you interested in the role of abolitionists in the war? In the events and ideas that led up to the Emancipation Proclamation? In what slaves thought about the war? List those questions and try to answer them as you read. As you begin to answer some of your initial questions, you will gain a deeper knowledge of your subject, and more detailed questions will arise: What role did freed slaves play in Union regiments? How were black soldiers treated by their white commanders? If you read actively in this way, you will discover which questions have been thoroughly discussed and which are less well studied. You will find the areas in which historians have reached consensus and questions that are still the subject of debate. Ultimately, you may even find an area where you feel you can say something both interesting and original.

Finally, write as you read. Most scholars would agree that reading and writing are interactive processes. Writing will help you clarify your thoughts about what you are reading and provide direction for your research.

MAKE AN OUTLINE. The preliminary writing that you do for your research paper—listing questions, taking notes, jotting down ideas, and so on—is intended to stimulate and clarify your thinking and thereby help you narrow your initial broad interests into a workable paper topic. The end result is the generation of a working thesis: a single sentence in which you state what you have concluded about your topic. (For a fuller discussion of the thesis, see pp. 29–32.) Once you know what argument you wish to make and have stated it in a working thesis, it is useful to sketch out the body of your paper in the form of an outline.

Some students have been trained to write formal outlines with roman numerals and various subheadings. If this method works for you, by all means use it. However, many students find formal outlines too constraining: one student said she can write such an outline only *after* her paper is written, which of course defeats the purpose.

The most important function of an outline is to provide a guide that notes the points you wish to cover and the order in which you plan to cover them. A good outline will help you present the evidence that supports your thesis as a convincing argument.

You might begin an informal outline by writing down the main points you want to discuss. These will form the topic sentences of paragraphs. Underneath each main point, list the evidence that supports it. Outlining your paper in this way will make readily apparent any points for which you lack sufficient evidence. It will also help ensure that your evidence is organized in a logical and orderly manner and that each idea is connected to those that precede and follow it.

NOTE: Remember that an outline is a *tool;* it is not divinely ordained nor fixed in stone. As you continue to think and write about your subject, you may discover new material or change your mind about the significance of certain material. You may even change your thesis (which is why your thesis at this stage is a *working* thesis rather than a final one). When this happens, you must be willing to revise your outline too.

DOCUMENT YOUR SOURCES. For a research paper, your professor will expect complete and accurate documentation of your sources. (See "Quoting and Documenting Sources" beginning on p. 41 for information on documentation.)

Revising your research paper

A research paper is a complex project. You need to analyze your sources, synthesize information, organize your thoughts, and present them in a coherent and persuasive manner. As with a short essay, you must construct an argument with a thesis and supporting evidence, but in the case of a research paper, you will need to analyze and synthesize much more material. You will probably have more counterevidence to address as well. It is unrealistic to expect that one or two drafts will be sufficient to do justice to the project. Give yourself time to revise your writing.

Following Conventions of Writing in History

Each academic discipline has its own practices, or conventions, that people writing in the discipline follow when engaged in a scholarly dialogue. These conventions are not hard-and-fast rules, but following them will make it easier for you to participate in an academic "conversation" in your field. Moreover, many historians are excellent stylists; your instructor will pay attention to your writing, so your attempts to learn and follow the conventions of the discipline will be noticed — and worth the effort. This section first looks at general conventions of writing history papers and then turns to concerns of word choice and grammar.

Considering the whole paper

Your relationship to your subject

When you write a history paper, you are not engaged in creative writing; rather, you are forming a relationship of sorts with real people and events whose integrity must be respected. It is useful to keep in mind several conventions historians have established for such relationships.

RESPECT YOUR SUBJECT. The people who lived in the past were not necessarily more ignorant or cruel (or, conversely, more innocent or moral) than we are. It is condescending, for example, to suggest that any intelligent or insightful person was "ahead of his or her time" (suggesting, of course, that he or she thought the same way we do).

DO NOT GENERALIZE. Remember that groups are formed of individuals. Do not assume that everyone who lived in the past believed the same things or behaved the same way. Avoid broad generalizations, such as "the Middle Ages was an age of faith." At best, such statements are clichés. More often than not, they are also wrong.

AVOID ANACHRONISM. An anachronistic statement is one in which an idea, event, person, or thing is represented in a way that is not consistent with its proper historical time. For example, "Despite the fact that bubonic plague can be controlled with antibiotics, medieval physicians treated their patients with ineffective folk remedies." This sentence includes two anachronisms. First, although antibiotics are effective against bubonic plague, they had not yet been discovered in the fourteenth century; it is anachronistic to mention them in a discussion of the Middle Ages. Second, it is anachronistic to judge medieval medicine by modern standards. A more effective discussion of the medieval response to the bubonic plague would focus on fourteenth-century knowledge about health and disease, theories of contagion, and sanitation practices.

In short, you should not import the values, beliefs, and practices of the present into the past. Try to understand the people and events of the past in their own contexts.

BE AWARE OF YOUR OWN BIASES. We naturally choose to write about subjects that interest us. Historians should not, however, let their own concerns and biases direct the way they interpret the past. A student of early modern Europe, for example, might be dismayed by the legal, social, and economic limitations placed on women in that period. Reproaching sixteenth-century men for being "selfish and chauvinistic" might forcefully express such a student's sense of indignation about what appears to modern eyes as unjust, but it is not a useful approach for the historian, who tries to understand the viewpoints of people in the past in the social context of the period under study.

The introduction and thesis

The introductory paragraph of your paper is in many ways the most important one and, therefore, the most difficult to write. In your introduction, you must (1) let your readers know what your paper is about, (2) put the topic of your paper into context, and (3) state your thesis — the position you are going to take on the topic. You must also attract your readers' attention and interest. The opening paragraph, then, has to frame the rest of the paper, and it has to make readers want to continue reading.

There is no magic formula for writing an effective first paragraph. You should, however, keep these conventions in mind.

DO NOT OPEN WITH A "GLOBAL" STATEMENT. Unsure of how to start, many students begin their papers with phrases like "Throughout history" or "From the beginning of time" or "People have always wondered about. . . ." You should avoid broad generalizations like these. First, you cannot prove that they are true: how do you know what people have always thought or done? Second, these statements are so broad that they are virtually meaningless; they offer no specific points or details to interest readers. Finally, such statements are so general that they give readers no clue about the subject of your paper. In general, it is much more effective to begin with material that is specific to your topic.

For example, the following opening sentence comes from a student's first draft of a paper on William Harvey, the seventeenth-century physician who discovered the circulation of blood:

> From ancient times, people have always been interested in the human body and how it works.

Although, strictly speaking, there is nothing wrong with this sentence, it is not a particularly effective opening. For one thing, it is such a general statement that readers will be inclined to ask, "So what?" In addition, it gives readers no indication of what the paper is about. Will the essay examine ancient Greek medical theory? Chinese acupuncture? Sex education in twentieth-century American schools?

In revising the sentence, the student eliminated the general statement altogether and began instead with a description of the intellectual context of Harvey's work:

> For the scholars and physicians of sixteenth-century Europe, observation and experimentation began to replace authoritative texts as the most important source of information about human anatomy and physiology.

From this short sentence, readers learn four things about the subject of the paper: the time frame of the discussion (the sixteenth century); the place (Europe); the people involved (scholars and physicians); and the topic (the relationship between authority and experience in the study of human physiology). Readers' curiosity is also piqued by the questions implied in the opening statement: Why did experimentation begin to replace authoritative texts? Was this change a subject of controversy? Who was involved? How did this change in method affect the science of biology and the practice of medicine? In other words, this opening sentence makes readers want to continue reading; they want to know the author's thesis.

INCLUDE YOUR THESIS IN THE FIRST PARAGRAPH. If your opening sentence has been effective, it will make your readers want to know the main point of your paper, which you will state in the *thesis*. The introduction to a journal article or book may be long, even several paragraphs, and the author's thesis may appear anywhere within it. Until you become very skilled in writing about history, however, it is best to keep your introduction short and to state your thesis in the first paragraph.

Your thesis must be more than a description of your topic or a statement of fact; it should inform readers of your interpretation of the materials you have read and the conclusions you have reached. The following is the first draft of a thesis statement from a student paper on Samuel George Morton, a nineteenth-century physician and scientist who wrote several influential treatises on craniometry, the nineteenth-century science of measuring the human skull:

> Morton measured the size and shape of human skulls from various racial and ethnic groups, concluding that Caucasians had the largest skulls and were therefore superior to all other races.

This is not really a thesis at all. While it is an accurate description of what Morton did, it does not tell readers anything they couldn't learn from the most cursory reading of one of Morton's books.

Now look at the revised version of the thesis:

> Morton and his contemporaries used his skull studies, which he said were objective and quantitative, to justify their belief in the superiority of the Caucasian race; however, a close examination of Morton's work reveals, as Stephen Jay Gould has suggested, that his supposedly scientific data were created by his own prejudices and racism.

This version of the thesis provides more than a simple description of what Morton did or said. Having studied Morton's works thoroughly and carefully, the writer has now come to a conclusion: that despite appearances to the contrary, Morton's studies were not scientific and his data-collecting procedures were biased by his prejudices. Moreover, this thesis also tells readers why the writer thinks his topic is historically significant: Morton's views are important because they provided his contemporaries with a seemingly scientific justification for racism. Finally, this thesis statement anticipates the type of argument that will follow: the paper will examine Morton's skull studies, discuss the ways in which they appear to be scientific, demonstrate the ways in which they are not scientific, and reveal the hidden biases and assumptions behind them. For all of these reasons, the revised thesis is much more effective than the draft thesis.

PLAN TO REWRITE YOUR OPENING PARAGRAPH. If you are having trouble beginning your paper, write a rough, temporary opening paragraph and return to it when you finish your first draft of the entire paper. The act of writing your draft will help you clarify your ideas, your topic, and your argument. It may also help solidify your thesis and your opening.

The body

In your introduction, you present your subject and state your thesis. In subsequent paragraphs, you provide evidence for your thesis and answer any objections that could be made to it. The following advice will help you to write well-organized paragraphs and make your argument clear and convincing.

BEGIN EACH PARAGRAPH WITH A TOPIC SENTENCE. Each paragraph should have one driving idea, which is usually asserted in the first sentence, or topic sentence. If you have made an outline, your topic sentences will be drawn from the list you made of the main points you wish to cover in your paper. (For advice on making an outline, see p. 26.)

MAKE CLEAR CONNECTIONS BETWEEN IDEAS. Each body paragraph provides evidence for your thesis in the form of examples, statistics, and so on. To be convincing, however, your evidence must be presented in a clear and well-organized way. Transitional words and phrases tell your readers how the individual statements in your paragraph are connected. To choose transitions that are appropriate, you will need to consider how your ideas are related to each other. Following is a list of transitional words or phrases that you might use to indicate particular kinds of relationships.

TO COMPARE:

also, similarly, likewise

TO CONTRAST:

on the other hand, although, nevertheless, despite, on the contrary, still, yet, regardless, nonetheless, notwithstanding, whereas, however, in spite of

TO ADD OR INTENSIFY:

also, in addition, moreover, furthermore, too, besides, and

TO SHOW SEQUENCE:

first (and any other numerical adjectives), last, next, finally, subsequently, later, ultimately

TO INDICATE AN EXAMPLE:

for example, for instance, specifically

TO INDICATE CAUSE-AND-EFFECT RELATIONSHIPS:

consequently, as a result, because, accordingly, thus, since, therefore, so

DO NOT WANDER OFF THE SUBJECT. If you include a lot of irrelevant information, you will lose momentum and your readers will lose the thread of your argument. Be ruthless: eliminate all extraneous material from the final draft of your paper, however interesting it may be. For instance, if you are writing about the role that Chinese laborers played in the westward expansion of the American railroads, do not spend three paragraphs discussing the construction of the steam locomotive. If your paper concerns the American government's treatment of Japanese citizens during World War II, do not digress into a discussion of naval tactics in the Pacific theater. Similarly, you should avoid repetition and wordy sentences.

Here is a paragraph from the first draft of a paper on Chinese relationships with foreigners during the Ming period:

The Chinese were willing to trade with barbarians. They distrusted foreigners. Jesuit missionaries were able to establish contacts in China. During the seventeenth century, they acquired the patronage of important officials.

They were the emperor's advisers. Chinese women bound their feet, a practice which many Europeans disliked. Relations between China and Europe deteriorated in the eighteenth century. The Jesuits were willing to accommodate themselves to Chinese culture. Chinese culture was of great interest to the scholars of Enlightenment Europe. Matteo Ricci learned about Chinese culture and became fluent in Mandarin. He adopted the robes of a Chinese scholar. He thought that Christianity was compatible with Confucianism. The Jesuit missionaries had scientific knowledge. In the eighteenth century, the papacy forbade Chinese Christians to engage in any form of ancestor worship.

This paragraph is very confusing. In the first place, there is no clear topic sentence; readers have to guess what the writer's main point is. This confusion is compounded by the fact that the connections between ideas are unclear; the paragraph lacks transitional words or phrases that alert readers to the connections that the writer sees between ideas or events. The paragraph is also poorly organized; the writer seems to move at random from topic to topic.

Here is a revised version of the same paragraph:

The Chinese of the Ming dynasty were deeply suspicious of foreigners; *nevertheless,* Jesuit missionaries were able to achieve positions of honor and trust in the imperial court, *ultimately* serving the emperor as scholars and advisers. *At first* glance, this phenomenon seems baffling; upon closer consideration, *however,* it becomes clear that the Jesuits' success was due to their willingness to accommodate themselves to Chinese culture. *For example,* one of the most successful of the early Jesuit missionaries, Matteo Ricci, steeped himself in Chinese culture *and* became fluent in Mandarin. To win the respect of the nobles, he *also* adopted the robes of a Chinese scholar. *Moreover,* he emphasized the similarities between Christianity and Chinese tradition. *Because* of their willingness to adapt to Chinese culture, Jesuit missionaries were accepted by the imperial court until the eighteenth century. Difficulties arose, *however,* when the papacy forbade Chinese Christians to engage in many traditional customs, including any form of ancestor worship. *As a result of* the church's increasing unwillingness to allow such practices, relations between China and Europe deteriorated.

This paragraph has been improved in several ways. First, a topic sentence has been added to the beginning; readers no longer need to guess that this paragraph will address the apparent contrast between sixteenth-century

Chinese suspicion of foreigners and the imperial court's acceptance of Jesuit missionaries.

Second, the author has elucidated the connections between ideas by including transitional words and phrases. These transitions, which have been italicized, illustrate several different kinds of relationships, including contrast, cause and effect, sequence, and so on, and allow readers to follow the writer's argument.

Third, the paragraph has been reorganized so that the relationships between events are clearer. For example, the revised paragraph states explicitly that relations between China and European missionaries deteriorated in the eighteenth century because the church became less accommodating to Chinese customs, a relationship obscured in the original paragraph by poor organization.

Finally, the writer has removed references to the practice of foot binding and to European interest in China during the Enlightenment. Both are interesting but irrelevant in a paragraph that deals with Chinese attitudes toward Europeans.

ANTICIPATE AND RESPOND TO COUNTEREVIDENCE AND COUNTERARGUMENTS. Historical issues are seldom clear-cut, and historians often disagree with one another. Effective papers acknowledge disagreement and differing viewpoints. If you discover information that does not support your thesis, do not suppress it. It is important to acknowledge *all* of your data. You should try to explain to your readers why your interpretation is valid, despite the existence of counterevidence, but do not imply that your interpretation is stronger than it is by eliminating data or falsifying your information.

A student writing about the French Revolution, for instance, might argue that the average Parisian worker became a revolutionary not as a result of reading the political arguments of the Enlightenment thinkers but rather from desperate economic need. But the student cannot ignore the fact that many Parisian workers had read such works and that Enlightenment thinkers were often quoted in the popular press. Rather, a successful paper would acknowledge these facts and attempt to show that economic need was a more important or more immediate catalyst for political action.

Remember, too, that it is important to treat opposing viewpoints with respect. It is perfectly legitimate to disagree with the interpretations of other historians. In disagreeing, however, you should never resort to name-calling, nor should you oversimplify or otherwise distort opposing points of view. It is important to understand opposing arguments and respond to them fairly.

The conclusion

Your paper should not come to an abrupt halt. Yet you do not need to conclude by summarizing everything that you have said in the body of the text. It is usually best to end your paper with a paragraph that states the most important conclusions you have reached about your subject and the reasons you think those conclusions are significant. You should avoid introducing new ideas or information in the conclusion. If an idea or fact is important to your argument, you should introduce and discuss it earlier; if it is not, you should leave it out altogether.

Considering word choice and grammar

Any good style guide or writing manual will offer plenty of advice for writing clear, grammatical sentences. (See Appendix A, p. 74, for a list of guides.) Following are some major points to keep in mind while writing in history.

Word choice

The words with which you choose to express yourself are a reflection of your own style. Nevertheless, here are a few guidelines.

AVOID CONVERSATIONAL LANGUAGE, SLANG, AND JARGON. Because history papers are usually formal, you should use formal language rather than conversational language and slang. For example, although it is perfectly acceptable in conversational English to say that someone "was a major player" in an event, this expression is too informal for a history paper. In addition, slang often sounds anachronistic: historians do not usually describe an aggressive individual as being "in your face"; people are "killed," not "bumped off." Words with double meanings should be used only in their conventional sense: use *cool* and *hot* to refer to temperature and *radical* to describe something extreme or on the political left. *Awesome* should generally be reserved for awe-inspiring things like Gothic cathedrals. You should also avoid jargon, or specialized language, which can often obscure your meaning.

MAKE YOUR LANGUAGE AS CLEAR AND SIMPLE AS POSSIBLE. In an effort to sound sophisticated, students sometimes use a thesaurus to find a "more impressive" word. The danger of this approach is that the new word might not mean quite what you intended. In general, you should use the simplest word that makes your meaning clear. Do not use a four-syllable word when a single syllable will do. Do not use five words (such as *due to the influence of*) where you can use one (*because*).

AVOID BIASED LANGUAGE. Always take care to avoid words that are gender-biased or that have negative connotations for particular racial, ethnic, or religious groups. Obviously, you should never use expressions that are clearly pejorative. In addition, however, you should be aware that many words that were once acceptable are now deemed inappropriate. For example, the use of masculine words or pronouns to refer to both men and women, once a common practice, is now termed "sexist" by many. Use *humankind* or *people* rather than *mankind,* and do not use a masculine pronoun to refer to people of both genders.

It is also important to realize that you cannot always rely on the books you are reading to alert you to biased language. For example, the author of a fairly recent study of the origins of racism consistently refers to Asian people as "Orientals," a term that was not generally thought derogatory at the time of the book's publication. Since then, however, the word *Oriental* has come to be seen as pejorative and should therefore not be used. Another example is the term *Negro,* which was once used to refer to people of African descent. Today, the preferred term is *black* or *African American.*

NOTE: You cannot, of course, correct the language of your sources; if you are quoting directly, you must use the exact wording of your source, including any racist or sexist language. If you are paraphrasing or summarizing, you might want to use nonbiased language instead of biased language when it doesn't distort the sense of the source. Otherwise, put biased terms in quotation marks to indicate to your readers that the words are your source's, not yours.

Tense

The events that historians write about took place in the past; therefore, historians conventionally use the past tense. Students are sometimes tempted to use the historical present tense for dramatic effect or to make the scene they are describing come alive, as in this example from a student paper:

> The battle rages all around him, but the squire is brave and acquits himself well. He defends his lord fearlessly and kills two of the enemy. As the fighting ends, he kneels before his lord on the battlefield, the bodies of the dead and dying all around him. His lord draws his sword and taps it against the squire's shoulders. The squire has proven his worth, and this is his reward; he is now a knight.

This use of the present may be a very effective device if you are writing fiction, but it is awkward in a history paper. First, readers might become confused about whether the events under discussion happened in the past or in the present, especially if the paper includes modern assessments of the issue. Second, use of the present makes it very easy for the writer to fall prey to anachronism (see p. 29). Perhaps more important, writing in the present sounds artificial; in normal conversation, we talk about events that happened in the past in the past tense. The same approach is also best for writing.

The present tense is used, however, when discussing the contents of documents, artifacts, or works of art because these still exist in the present. Note, for example, the appropriate use of past and present tenses in the following description:

> Columbus sailed across an "ocean sea" far greater than he initially imagined. The admiral's *Journal* tells us what Columbus thought he would find: a shorter expanse of water, peppered with hundreds of hospitable islands.

The events of the past are referred to in the past tense (*sailed, imagined, thought*), and the contents of the *Journal* are referred to in the present (*tells*).

Voice

In general, historians prefer the active rather than the passive voice. In the active voice, the subject of the sentence is also the actor:

Duke William of Normandy conquered England in 1066.

By the seventh century, the Chinese had invented gunpowder, which they used to make fireworks.

Emperor Gia Long, with French military and naval support, united Vietnam in 1802.

In the passive voice, the subject of the sentence is not the actor but is acted upon:

England was conquered in 1066.

The process for making gunpowder was known in the seventh century.

Vietnam was united in 1802.

There are several difficulties with using the passive voice. Persistent use of the passive voice can make writing sound dull. More important, however, use of the passive voice can often obscure meaning and create unnecessary confusion. And as you can see from these examples, readers cannot always tell who the actor is. We are not told, for example, who conquered England or who invented gunpowder.

Use of the passive voice also allows writers to avoid the complexities of some historical issues. In the second example, for instance, moving from the passive to the active voice forces the writer to be more specific; the Chinese invented gunpowder, but they used it for making fireworks, not in weapons. Similarly, in the third example, use of the active voice makes the writer think about *who* united Vietnam in 1802, which leads to a consideration of the relationship between Emperor Gia Long and the French military in bringing about that unity.

In addition, use of the passive voice in the expressions "it can be argued that" or "it has been argued that" is equivocal. The first expression suggests that the writer is unwilling to take responsibility for his or her arguments. If your evidence leads you to a certain conclusion, state it clearly; using passive expressions like "it can be argued that" suggests that you are not really sure that your evidence is convincing. Similarly, the expression "it has been argued that" confuses readers: Who has made this argument? How many people and in what context? Readers must have this information to evaluate your argument. Moreover, use of this expression can result in plagiarism. If someone or several persons have argued a particular point, you should identify them, in your text itself and in a citation.

This is not to say, however, that you should never use the passive voice. Here, for example, is a description of the Holocaust (verbs in the passive voice have been italicized):

Hitler engaged in the systematic and ruthless murder of the Jewish people. In 1933, Jews *were forbidden* to hold public office; by 1935, they *were deprived* of citizenship. In all, over six million Jews *were killed* as part of Hitler's "final solution."

In this passage, the writer wants to draw readers' attention to the recipients of the action — the six million Jews killed in the Holocaust. The persons acted upon are more important than the actor. The passive voice, which focuses attention on the victims, is therefore appropriate here.

The passive voice, then, can be effective; but it should be used only occasionally and for a specific reason.

Use of the pronouns I, me, and you

Until recently, most professional historians used the pronouns *I, me,* and *you* sparingly, if at all. This convention has been changing, however, and these pronouns are beginning to appear more regularly in history books and journal articles. Although many instructors still prefer that students avoid personal pronouns whenever possible, an increasing number of professors find their use not only acceptable but actually preferable to more labored constructions like "this evidence leads one to conclude that." Since the conventions governing the use of personal pronouns are in flux, it is best to consult your instructor about his or her preferences.

NOTE: When you are writing a book review, it is unnecessary to preface statements with *I think* or *in my opinion* since it is conventional to assume that as a reviewer you are expressing your own opinions.

Quoting and Documenting Sources

Any history paper you write will be the result of your careful reading and analysis of primary and secondary sources. This section offers general guidance in incorporating source material into your writing through paraphrase and quotation. It also explains the conventions historians use to cite and document sources and will help you avoid the very serious offense of plagiarism.

Using quotations

Quotations are an important part of writing in history. Quotations from primary sources provide evidence and support for your thesis. Quotations from secondary sources tell your readers that you are well informed about the current state of research on the issue about which you are writing. However, some students go to extremes, producing papers that are little more than a series of quotations loosely strung together. No matter how interesting and accurate the quotations, such a paper is no substitute for your own analysis and discussion of sources. In general, you should minimize your use of quotations, and you should choose the quotations you do use with great care.

The following guidelines will help you to decide when to quote and how to use quotations effectively.

DO NOT QUOTE IF YOU CAN PARAPHRASE. Summarizing or paraphrasing in your own words is usually preferable to direct quotation; it demonstrates that you have digested the information from the source and made it your own. In particular, you should not quote directly if the quotation would provide only factual information. Look at this passage from Bede's *Ecclesiastical History*, followed by a paraphrase.

ORIGINAL PASSAGE

When our holy father Augustine, the beloved of God, died, his body was laid to rest at the entrance to the church of the holy Apostles Peter and Paul, since the church was not yet completed or consecrated. But as soon as it was dedicated, his body was brought inside and buried in the north porch with great honour.[1]

PARAPHRASE

According to Bede, St. Augustine's burial had to be delayed because the church of Sts. Peter and Paul was still under construction at the time of his death.

Because the original passage is merely factual and not especially striking, the paraphrase would be preferable in a student paper.

DO QUOTE IF THE WORDS OF THE ORIGINAL ARE ESPECIALLY MEMORABLE. You might want to quote directly when your source says something in a particularly striking way. Read the following passage from the "Letter to the Grand Duchess Christina," in which Galileo argues that scriptural passages that describe physical phenomena need not be interpreted literally since the Bible is not a scientific text:

> Now if the Holy Spirit has purposely neglected to teach us propositions of this sort [i.e., physical propositions] as irrelevant to the highest goal (that is, our salvation), how can anyone affirm that it is obligatory to take sides on them, and that one belief is required by faith, while the other side is erroneous? Can an opinion be heretical and yet have no concern with the salvation of souls? . . . I would say here something that was heard from an ecclesiastic of the most eminent degree: "That the intention of the Holy Ghost is to teach us how one goes to heaven, not how heaven goes."[2]

The quotation from the "eminent ecclesiastic" is memorable because of the play on words, which could not be duplicated in a summary or paraphrase. Galileo, then, chose an effective quotation.

You might also wish to quote when the original words are important to readers' understanding of the author's intentions or feelings. Look at the following passage from Plato's *Apology.* The speaker is Socrates; he is addressing the jurors who have just condemned him to death.

---

1. Bede, *Ecclesiastical History of the English People,* trans. Leo Sherley Price, 1955; rev. ed. R. E. Latham (Harmondsworth, England: Penguin, 1990), 180.

2. Galileo Galilei, "Letter to Madame Christina of Lorraine, Grand Duchess of Tuscany" in *Discoveries and Opinions of Galileo,* trans. with intro. and notes by Stillman Drake (New York: Doubleday, 1957), 185–86.

> This much I ask from you: when my sons grow up, avenge
> yourselves by causing them the same kind of grief that I
> caused you. . . . Reproach them as I reproach you, that they
> do not care for the right things and think they are worthy
> when they are not worthy of anything. If you do this, I shall
> have been justly treated by you, and my sons also.[3]

In this passage, the tone is as important as the content. It
would be impossible to capture in a summary or paraphrase
the irony of the original.

Conventions for using quotations

When you quote, you must follow the conventions for using
quotation marks and integrating quotations in the text of
your paper. Following are some important points to keep in
mind.

INDICATE WHERE YOUR QUOTATION BEGINS AND ENDS. If you
quote a source, you should quote the source's words *exactly*,
and you should enclose the material from your source in quotation marks. If your quotation is more than four typed lines,
you should set the quotation off by indenting it; this is called
a *block quotation*. Typically, long quotations are preceded by
an introductory sentence followed by a colon. You should use
block quotations very sparingly, if at all. Frequent use of long
quotations suggests that you have not really understood the
material well enough to paraphrase (see p. 41). Moreover, a
long quotation can be distracting, causing readers to lose the
thread of your argument. You should therefore use a lengthy
quotation only if you have a compelling reason to do so.

NOTE: Professional editors prefer that block quotations be
double-spaced. It has become conventional, however, for
block quotations to be single-spaced in student papers. Ask
your instructor which form he or she prefers.

KEEP QUOTATIONS BRIEF. To keep quoted material to a mini-
mum, you should condense quoted passages by using the
ellipsis mark (three periods, with spaces between), which
indicates that you have left out some of the original material.
The preceding quotation from Plato's *Apology* is an example
of this method.

---

3. Plato, *Apology*, in *Five Dialogues*, trans. G. M. A. Grube (Indianapolis: Hackett Publishing Company, 1981), 44.

FRAME YOUR QUOTATION. Quotations from sources cannot simply be dropped into your paper; even if a quotation is appropriate to a point you are making, you cannot assume that its significance is immediately obvious to your readers. You should always make it clear to your readers how the quotation you have chosen supports your argument. This example is from a student paper on Judge Benjamin Lindsey, the founder of the first juvenile court in the United States:

> Like most progressives, Lindsey was interested in social reform. "I found no 'problem of the children' that was not also the problem of their parents."[4]

It is not clear how the quotation from Lindsey illustrates the writer's statement that Lindsey was interested in social reform. Are readers meant to assume that Lindsey wanted to remove children from the homes of unfit parents? Provide government support for indigent parents? Encourage state-funded family counseling?

In the revised version, the student frames the quotation in a way that makes its significance clear:

> Noting that youthful offenders were often the product of criminal environments, Lindsey argued that even the most vigorous attempts to curb juvenile delinquency would fail until more sweeping social reforms eliminated the economic and social factors that led their parents to engage in illegal activities. Addressing the need to rehabilitate and reeducate adult criminals, he wrote: "I found no 'problem of the children' that was not also the problem of their parents." Thus, for Lindsey, the reform of the juvenile justice system was intrinsically linked to the reform of adult criminal courts.

In this revision, the significance of the quotation as it pertains to the writer's argument is clear. The writer's analysis before and after the quotation puts Lindsey's words in context.

Avoiding plagiarism

Plagiarism is a *very* serious academic offense. The penalties for plagiarism are usually severe, ranging from an automatic F in the course to temporary suspension or even permanent expulsion from the university. In some circumstances, plagia-

4. Benjamin Barr Lindsey, *The Beast* (New York: Doubleday, 1910), 151.

rism may even be a crime. Although some individuals deliberately copy lengthy passages or even purchase whole papers, most student plagiarism stems not from dishonest intent but from lack of understanding about what exactly constitutes plagiarism. Most unintentional plagiarism can be traced to three sources: uncertainty about how to paraphrase; confusion about when and how to cite sources; and carelessness in taking notes and downloading Internet materials.

Paraphrasing to avoid plagiarism

Most students know that copying a passage word for word from a source is plagiarism. However, many are unsure about how to paraphrase. Consider, for example, this passage from a textbook and the student "paraphrase" that follows:

ORIGINAL PASSAGE

In the early twentieth century, most Latin American nations were characterized by two classes separated by a great gulf. At the top were a small group of European-descended white people, the *patrones* (landlords or patrons), who, along with foreign investors, owned the ranches, mines and plantations of each nation. Like the established families of most societies elsewhere in the world, the *patrones* monopolized the wealth, social prestige, education, and cultural attainments of their nations. Many of them aspired to the ideal of nobility, with high standards of personal morality and a parental concern for those who worked for them. Some *patrones* lived up to these ideals, but most, consciously or unconsciously, exploited their workers.[5]

UNSUCCESSFUL "PARAPHRASE"

In the early part of this century most Latin American countries were typified by two classes separated by a large chasm. At the top were a small group of white people, descended from Europeans, called *patrones*. Along with foreign investors, the *patrones* owned the plantations, ranches, and mines of their countries. Like aristocrats all over the world, the *patrones* controlled the wealth, social status, education, and cultural achievements of their countries. Many of them had high standards of morality and were concerned for their workers, but most, consciously or unconsciously, abused their workers.

5. Richard Goff, Walter Moss, Janice Terry, and Jiu-Hwa Upshur, *The Twentieth Century: A Brief Global History*, 4th ed. (New York: McGraw-Hill, 1994), 62.

In this example, the writer's attempt at paraphrase results in plagiarism, *despite the fact* that the second text is not an exact copy of the original. The writer has used a thesaurus to find synonyms for several words — *characterized* has become *typified, gulf* has been replaced by *chasm,* and *achievements* has been substituted for *attainments.* In addition, several words or phrases in the original have been left out in the second version, and the word order has occasionally been rearranged. Nevertheless, these changes are merely editorial; the new paragraph is not significantly different from the original in either form or substance.

NOTE: This paragraph would be considered plagiarism *even if* the writer acknowledged the source of the material; it is simply too close to the original to be considered the work of the student.

In a genuine paraphrase, the writer has thought about what the source says and digested it; once the writer understands the content of the source, he or she can restate it in an entirely original way that reflects his or her own wording and style. Consider, for example, this paraphrase:

PARAPHRASE

The society of Latin America at the beginning of this century was sharply divided into two groups: the vast majority of the population, made up of the workers, and a wealthy minority, the *patrones,* who were descended from white Europeans. Although the *patrones* represented a very small segment of the population, they controlled the lion's share of their countries' wealth and enjoyed most of the social and educational advantages. Like their counterparts in Europe, many *patrones* adopted an attitude of paternalistic benevolence toward those who worked for them. Even if their concern was genuine, however, the *patrones* clearly reaped the rewards of their workers' labor.

This paraphrase is more successful; the writer has assimilated the content of the source and expressed it in his own words.

NOTE: You will save time if you paraphrase as you take notes. However, if you attempt to paraphrase with the original source open in front of you, you are courting disaster. To write a genuine paraphrase, you should close the book and rewrite in your own words what you have read. (For advice on taking notes in the form of summaries, see p. 23. A shorter example of paraphrasing can be found on p. 42.)

Citing sources to avoid plagiarism

When you derive facts and ideas from other writers' work, you must cite the sources of your information. Most writers are aware that they must cite the sources of direct quotations, but you must also provide citations for *all* information derived from another source, even if you have summarized or paraphrased the information. You must also cite your sources when you use other writers' interpretations of a historical event or text. Citing sources enables your readers to distinguish between your ideas and those of others.

The only exception is that you do not need to provide citations for information that is common knowledge. For example, you might have learned from a particular book that the Civil War spanned the years 1861–65, but you do not have to cite the book when you include this fact in your paper. You could have obtained the time span of the Civil War from any number of sources because it is common knowledge. The more you read about your subject, the easier it will be for you to distinguish common knowledge from information for which you need to provide a citation. When in doubt, it is better to be safe and cite the source.

Downloading Internet sources carefully

As with any other source, information derived from the Internet must be properly paraphrased and cited. A particular danger arises, however, from the ease with which Internet material can be downloaded into your working text. Whenever you download material from the Internet, be sure to create *a separate document file* for that material. Otherwise, Internet material may inadvertently become mixed up with your own writing.

Documenting sources

For all of the sources in your paper, you must provide complete bibliographic information. This enables readers to look up your sources to evaluate your interpretation of them or to read more extensively from them.

Footnotes or endnotes

Historians usually use footnotes or endnotes to document their sources. With this method, you place a raised number, called a *superscript,* at the end of the last word of a quotation, paraphrase, or summary. This number corresponds to a numbered note that provides bibliographic information about your source. Notes may be placed at the bottom of the page (footnotes) or at the end of the paper (endnotes). In either case, notes should be numbered consecutively from the beginning to the end of the paper.

The following example shows a source cited in the text of a paper and documented in a footnote or endnote.

TEXT

Spurlock notes that when mesmerism came to America in 1836, "it was a method of curing sickness — a scientific triumph over magic."[3]

NOTE

3. John C. Spurlock, *Free Love: Marriage and Middle-Class Radicalism in America, 1825–1860* (New York: New York University Press, 1988), 85.

You should ask your instructor if he or she has a preference for footnotes or endnotes. If the choice is left up to you, weigh the advantages and disadvantages of each form. Footnotes allow your readers to refer easily and quickly to the sources cited on a given page, but they can be distracting. Further, historians often use explanatory or discursive notes, which contain more than simple bibliographic information. If your paper has a large number of such footnotes in addition to bibliographic footnotes, the pages might look overwhelmed with notes. If you use endnotes, you do not need to worry about the length of your notes. However, endnotes are less accessible, requiring readers to turn to the end of the paper to refer to each note.

Bibliography

Papers with footnotes or endnotes also have a bibliography, a list of all the sources cited in the paper, arranged alphabetically by authors' last names (or by title where there is no author). In a paper with endnotes, the bibliography always follows the last endnote page. (See pp. 72–73 for a sample bibliography.)

The author-date method

An alternative form of documentation that is becoming increasingly common in professional journals in the social sciences is the author-date system. The author's last name and the publication date of a cited source are included in parentheses in the text itself; complete bibliographic information appears in a reference list at the end of the text. This form of documentation is almost never used in history. In the first place, this system does not allow the writer to use explanatory or discursive notes. In addition, the author–date system is generally not practical for documenting many of the primary sources historians use. Occasionally, a professor may suggest the use of the author–date system for a book review or for a paper citing only one or two sources, but you should not use it unless you are specifically told to do so.

Documenting online sources

The Internet is an increasingly important tool for historical research. Since it is a relatively new tool, however, the conventions for documenting online sources are not yet firmly established. Nevertheless, it is essential that you provide your reader with enough information to locate and examine the material you have obtained from the Internet.

One useful source of information for documenting electronic sources is *Online! A Reference Guide to Using Internet Sources* by Andrew Harnack and Eugene Kleppinger (New York: St. Martin's Press, 1997). Documentation models for Internet and other electronic sources can also be found in this manual on pages 62–63 and 71.

Using quotations and documenting sources: A sample paragraph

A well-written paragraph incorporates and documents the use of source material. In the following paragraph, the writer has further revised her paragraph on page 34 to include short quotations, block quotations, citations of both primary and secondary sources, and a discursive footnote.

> The Chinese of the Ming dynasty were generally "uninterested in, and at times hostile to, things foreign."[6] The comments of one Ming official, Chang Han, reflect the attitude of many of his contemporaries:

---

6. John K. Fairbank and Edwin O. Reischauer, *China: Tradition and Transformation*, rev. ed. (Boston: Houghton Mifflin, 1989), 179.

> Foreigners are recalcitrant and their greed knows no
> bounds. . . . What is more, the greedy heart is unpre-
> dictable. If one day they break the treaties and invade
> our frontiers, who will be able to defend us against
> them?[7]

Despite this distrust, Jesuit missionaries were able to
achieve positions of honor and trust in the imperial court,
ultimately serving the emperor as scholars and advisers. It
seems clear that the Jesuits' success in establishing cordial
relations with the Chinese court was due to their initial
willingness to accommodate themselves to Chinese culture.
For example, realizing the extent to which the Chinese distrusted foreigners, one of the most successful of the early
Jesuit missionaries, Matteo Ricci, steeped himself in Chinese culture and became fluent in Mandarin. Recognizing
the importance of converting the highly educated members
of the court,[8] Ricci adopted the robes of a Chinese scholar.[9]
Moreover, he emphasized the similarities between Christianity and Chinese tradition, presenting Christianity as "a
system of wisdom and ethics compatible with Confucianism."[10] Because of their willingness to adapt to Chinese culture, Jesuit missionaries were accepted by the imperial
court until the eighteenth century. Difficulties arose, however, when the papacy forbade Chinese Christians to
engage in many traditional customs, including any form of
ancestor worship.[11] As the church became less accommodating to Chinese culture, relations between China and
Europe deteriorated.

Documentation models:
Notes and bibliographic entries

Following are models of notes and bibliographic entries for
the types of sources commonly used in history. The models
follow *The Chicago Manual of Style,* 14th ed. (Chicago: University of Chicago Press, 1993). Your professor will probably
tell you which style guide to use. (Many instructors ask their

---

7. Chang Han, "Essay on Merchants," trans. Lily Hwa, in *Chinese
Civilization and Society: A Sourcebook,* ed. Patricia Buckley Ebrey (New
York: Free Press, 1981), 157.

8. For a discussion of important converts to Christianity among
educated Chinese, see Jacques Gernet, *A History of Chinese Civilization,*
trans. J. R. Foster and Charles Hartman, 2d ed. (Cambridge: Cambridge
University Press, 1996), 456–58.

9. Gernet, 450.

10. Fairbank and Reischauer, 245.

11. Gernet, 519; Fairbank and Reischauer, 249.

students to use Kate L. Turabian's *A Manual for Writers,* which follows *The Chicago Manual of Style.*) Whatever style you use, it is important to be consistent: if your first footnote or endnote follows the *Chicago Manual* form, all of your notes and your bibliography must follow the *Chicago Manual.*

NOTE: Notes and bibliographies follow different forms. Models for notes are given first; bibliographic entries for the same sources begin on page 63.

Models for footnotes or endnotes

Books

A typical note for a book includes the following information:

- The author's full name (or the editor's full name, if no author is listed), followed by a comma
- The full title of the book, underlined or italicized
- Publication information: the city of publication, followed by a colon; the name of the publisher, followed by a comma; and the date of publication — all enclosed in parentheses and followed by a comma (*Note:* Well-known cities do not need to be followed by state names, and "Inc.," "Co.," and other such abbreviations may be dropped from publishers' names.)
- The page or pages cited, followed by a period

Individual entries should be single-spaced; double-space between notes. Typically, the first line of each note is indented.

BASIC FORM FOR A BOOK

    1. Marjorie Spruill Wheeler, *Votes for Women: The Woman Suffrage Movement in Tennessee, the South, and the Nation* (Knoxville: University of Tennessee Press, 1995), 44–46.

SHORTENED FORMS IN SUBSEQUENT REFERENCES

The first time you cite a work, you must provide complete bibliographic information. In subsequent references, however, you can use a shortened form. There are two acceptable methods to shorten a reference. You can cite the author's last name followed by a comma and the page or pages cited.

    2. Wheeler, 50.

If you cite more than one work by the same author in your paper or if a subsequent reference appears long after the first reference, you must include a shortened form of the title in your subsequent reference. To shorten the title, use the key word or words from the title of the book or article.

> 3. Wheeler, *New Women,* 114.

ABBREVIATIONS IN SUBSEQUENT REFERENCES

Ibid.   The abbreviation "ibid." (from the Latin *ibidem,* meaning "in the same place") is sometimes used to refer to the work cited in the previous note. However, many professors and professional journals prefer shortened second references; make sure you know which method your professor prefers.

When it is used, "ibid." stands in place of both the author's name and the title of the work. If you are referring to the same page, use "ibid." alone. If you are referring to different page numbers, use "ibid." followed by a comma and the new page numbers.

> 4. Ibid., 79–84.

NOTE: Never use "ibid." if the previous note refers to more than one work.

Idem   If you are citing several works by the same author within the same note, you can use the word "idem" (Latin for "the same") in place of the author's name after the first reference.

> 5. Samuel Brunk, *Revolution and Betrayal: A Life of Emiliano Zapata* (Albuquerque: University of New Mexico Press, 1995), 288; idem, "The Sad Situation of Civilians and Soldiers': The Banditry of Zapatismo in the Mexican Revolution," *American Historical Review* 101 (1996): 342.

Op. cit. and loc. cit.   The *Chicago Manual* discourages the use of either "op. cit." (meaning "in the work cited") or "loc. cit." ("in the place cited") to refer to the title of a work cited earlier. Use the shortened form instead.

TWO OR MORE AUTHORS

If a book has two or more authors, list the authors in your note in the same order in which their names appear on the title page.

6. Blanche Linden-Ward and Carol Hurd Green, *American Women in the 1960s: Changing the Future* (New York: Twayne, 1993), 92–93.

7. Joyce Appleby, Lynn Hunt, and Margaret Jacob, *Telling the Truth about History* (New York: Norton, 1994), 249.

NOTE: For books with more than three authors, you may use the Latin term "et al." ("and others") after the first author instead of listing all the authors (for example, "Jane Doe et al.").

AUTHOR'S NAME IN THE TITLE

Sometimes an author's name appears in the title of a book, as in an autobiography or a collection of letters or papers. In this case, your footnote or endnote should begin with the title of the book.

8. Darwin, Charles, *Charles Darwin's Letters: A Selection, 1825–1859,* ed. Frederick Burkhardt (Cambridge: Cambridge University Press, 1996), 15–19.

ANONYMOUS WORK

If the author of a work is unknown and if there is no editor or compiler, begin your note with the title.

9. *Images of America: A Panorama of History in Photographs* (Washington, D.C.: Smithsonian Books, 1989), 74.

EDITED OR COMPILED WORK WITHOUT AN AUTHOR

Cite a book by its editor (abbreviated "ed.") or compiler (abbreviated "comp.") if no author appears on the title page (as in a collection or anthology).

10. Gyan Prakash, ed., *After Colonialism: Imperial Histories and Postcolonial Displacements* (Princeton: Princeton University Press, 1995), 9.

EDITED WORK WITH AN AUTHOR

If an author's name is provided in addition to an editor's, give the editor's name after the title.

11. Frida Kahlo, *The Letters of Frida Kahlo: Cartas Apasionadas,* ed. Martha Zamora (San Francisco: Chronicle Books, 1995), 55.

TRANSLATED WORK

A translator's name, like an editor's, is placed after the title
when an author's name is given. If a source has an editor
and a translator, both should be listed.

> 12. Hector Aguilar Camin and Lorenzo Meyer, *In the
> Shadow of the Mexican Revolution: Contemporary Mexican
> History, 1910–1989,* trans. Luis Alberto Fierro (Austin: Uni-
> versity of Texas Press, 1993), 102–106.

> 13. Gerard Noiriel, *The French Melting Pot: Immigra-
> tion, Citizenship, and National Identity,* ed. Charles Tilly,
> trans. Geoffroy de Laforcade (Minneapolis: University of
> Minnesota Press, 1996), 88.

MULTIVOLUME WORK

If you cite a whole work that is published in multiple volumes, include the total number of volumes after the title.

> 14. *Freedom: A Documentary History of Emancipation,
> 1861–1867,* 4 vols. (New York: Cambridge University Press,
> 1993).

You can cite a single volume in a multivolume work in
one of two ways. You can give the name of the volume first,
or you can give the series name first.

> 15. *The Wartime Genesis of Free Labor: The Upper
> South,* ed. Ira Berlin, vol. 1 of *Freedom: A Documentary His-
> tory of Emancipation, 1861–1867* (New York: Cambridge
> University Press, 1993), 321–23.

or

> 15. *Freedom: A Documentary History of Emancipation,
> 1861–1867,* vol. 1, *The Wartime Genesis of Free Labor: The
> Upper South,* ed. Ira Berlin (New York: Cambridge University
> Press, 1993), 321–23.

If an individual volume of a multivolume work does not
have its own title, include the volume number and the page
numbers after the publication information.

> 16. *Cambridge History of American Foreign Relations*
> (Cambridge: Cambridge University Press, 1993), 1:32–33.

ARTICLE IN A COLLECTION OR ANTHOLOGY

If you cite an article in a collection or anthology, include both
the author and the title of the article, followed by the title,
editor, and publication information for the book in which it

appears. Also give the page or pages on which the information you are citing appears.

>   17. Wini Breines, "The 'Other' Fifties: Beats and Bad Girls," in *Not June Cleaver: Women and Gender in Post-War America, 1945–1960* (Philadelphia: Temple University Press, 1994), 382.

LETTER IN A PUBLISHED COLLECTION

When citing a letter that appears in a published collection, list the sender, recipient, and the date of the communication. Then cite the collection in the usual way.

>   18. Eugene V. Debs to John Reed, 21 September 1918, *Gentle Rebel: Letters of Eugene V. Debs*, ed. J. Robert Constantine (Urbana: University of Illinois Press, 1994), 110.

EDITION OTHER THAN THE FIRST

If the text you are using is not the first edition, provide the edition number in your note.

>   19. Hughes, Jonathan R., *American Economic History*, ed. Thomas Dublin, 4th ed. (New York: HarperCollins, 1994), 82.

WORK IN A SERIES

Some books are part of a series: publications on the same general subject that are supervised by a general editor or group of editors. The series title may be eliminated from your note if the book can be located easily without it. If a series editor is named, include this information after the series title.

>   20. Steven C. Hughes, *Crime, Disorder, and the Risorgimento: The Politics of Policing in Bologna*, Cambridge Studies in Italian History and Culture, ed. Giorgio Chittolini, vol. 4 (Cambridge: Cambridge University Press, 1994), 50–55.

Periodicals

A typical note for an article in a journal includes the following information:

- The author's full name, followed by a comma
- The title of the article, in quotation marks and followed by a comma
- The name of the journal in which the article appears, underlined or italicized
- The volume number (in arabic numerals, even if the journal uses roman numerals)

• The date, in parentheses, followed by a colon
• The page or pages cited, followed by a period

ARTICLE IN A JOURNAL PAGINATED BY VOLUME

Most scholarly journals are paginated consecutively through-out the volume. When citing an article from such a journal, it is not mandatory that you give the issue number, although this information may be useful, especially for recent, unbound journals.

> 21. Sarah Hanley, "Social Sites of Political Practice in France: Lawsuits, Civil Rights, and the Separation of Pow-ers in Domestic and State Government, 1500–1800," *Amer-ican Historical Review* 102 (1997): 27–29.

ARTICLE IN A JOURNAL PAGINATED BY ISSUE

If a journal paginates each issue separately, you must pro-vide the issue number. The following model is one of several acceptable forms for citing the issue of a journal. In this example, the volume number is 30, the issue number is 2, the year of publication is 1996, and the page reference is 47.

> 22. Sherrie A. Inness, "On the Road and in the Air: Gender and Technology in Girls' Automobile and Airplane Serials, 1909–1932," *Journal of Popular Culture* 30, no. 2 (1996): 47.

NOTE: If you wish to include the month of publication, put it before the year: (March 1986). If you include the month, you do not need the issue number.

ARTICLE IN A POPULAR MAGAZINE

In citing an article from a popular magazine, include the author, title of the article, magazine title, and date (not in parentheses). Omit the volume and issue numbers. It is not necessary to include page numbers; if you do include them, they should be preceded by a comma, not a colon.

> 23. Tom Engelhardt, "Fifty Years under a Cloud: The Uneasy Search for Our Atomic History," *Harper's,* January 1996, 76.

NEWSPAPER ARTICLE

When referring to an article in a daily newspaper, always cite the date, month, and year. Include the author's name, if it is given, and the title of the article. Each issue of a news-paper may go through several editions, and in each edition articles may be rearranged or even eliminated entirely. For this reason, you should cite the name of the edition in which the article appeared (for example, first edition, late edition). Page numbers are usually omitted. If you are citing a large newspaper that is published in sections, include the name, letter, or number of the section.

> 24. Rochelle Riley, "Black History Museum Focuses on Past and Future," *Louisville Courier-Journal,* 14 October 1997, sec. A.

NOTE: If the city of the newspaper is not well known, include the state in parentheses.

BOOK REVIEW

To cite a book review, begin with the reviewer's name followed by the title of the review, if one is given. Follow this information by the words "review of," the title of the work being reviewed, and its author. Also cite the periodical in which the review appears and the relevant publication information. If the author of the review is not named, begin with the title of the review or, if the review is untitled, with the words "Review of."

> 25. Candace Falk, review of *Better Red: The Writing and Resistance of Tillie Olsen and Meridel Le Sueur,* by Constance Coiner. *American Historical Review* 102 (1997): 208–9.

> 26. Review of *The Clash: A History of U.S.-Japan Relations,* by Walter LeFeber, *Publishers Weekly,* 21 July 1997, 193.

Public documents

In the United States, most federal government publications are printed by the Government Printing Office in Washington, D.C., and may be issued by both houses of Congress (the House of Representatives and the Senate); by the executive departments (for example, the Department of State, the Department of the Interior, and so on); or by government commissions or agencies (for example, the Securities and Exchange Commission). In addition, public documents may be issued by state or local governments. A reference to a public document should include the following:

- The name of the country, state, city, or county from which the document was issued (papers on United States history may omit "United States" or "U.S."

- The name of the legislative body, court, executive department, or other agency issuing the document
- The title of the document or collection, if given
- The name of the author, editor, or compiler
- The report number
- The publisher, if applicable ("Government Printing Office" may be shortened to "GPO")
- The date
- The page or pages cited

Following are models for notes citing government documents commonly used by students writing history papers.

PRESIDENTIAL PAPERS

The Government Printing Office has published the papers of the presidents of the United States in two multivolume collections: *Compilation of the Messages and Papers of the Presidents, 1789–1897* for the early presidency and *Public Papers of the Presidents of the United States* for twentieth-century presidents.

27. Dwight D. Eisenhower, *Public Papers of the Presidents of the United States: Dwight D. Eisenhower, 1953,* (Washington, D.C.: GPO, 1960), 228–30.

EXECUTIVE DEPARTMENT DOCUMENT

A note for a document issued by one of the executive departments begins with the issuing department. Include the name of the author of the document, if it is known. If the publication is part of a series, you may include the series number and omit the publication information.

28. U.S. General Accounting Office, *Desert Shield and Desert Storm Reports and Testimonies, 1991–93* (Washington, D.C.: General Accounting Office, 1994), 446.

29. U.S. Department of State, *Belarus,* Background Notes Series, no. 10344, 77.

TESTIMONY BEFORE A COMMITTEE

Transcripts of testimony presented before congressional committees or commissions can be found in records called "hearings." Begin the note with the committee or commission name.

30. House Committee on Veterans' Affairs, *Radiation Research in the VA Involving Human Subjects: Hearing before the Committee on Veterans' Affairs,* 103d Cong., 2d sess., 1994, 367.

CONGRESSIONAL COMMITTEE PRINT

Both houses of Congress issue research reports called "Committee Prints." Your note should include either the date or the Committee Print number, if one is provided.

> 31. U.S. Congress, Senate Committee on Foreign Relations, *Russia on the Eve of the Presidential Election: A Staff Report to the Committee on Foreign Relations,* 104th Cong., 2d sess., 1996, 244.

TREATY

Treaties can be found in volumes of *United States Treaties and Other International Agreements,* issued by the Government Printing Office. Each treaty in the bound volume was originally published in pamphlet form in a State Department series titled Treaties and Other International Acts (TIAS). In your note, the title (in quotation marks) and date of a treaty should follow the name of the issuing agency (such as U.S. Department of State). The number assigned to the treaty in TIAS is given in the bound volume and should also be included in your note.

> 32. U.S. Department of State, "Jay Treaty," 19 November 1794, TIAS no. 105, *United States Treaties and Other International Agreements,* vol. 2, 245.

UNITED STATES CONSTITUTION

The Constitution is cited by article (abbreviated "art.") or amendment ("amend.") and section ("sec.").

> 33. U.S. Constitution, art. 4, sec. 1.

The forms of notes for state and local government publications are essentially the same as those for federal government publications.

Other sources

UNPUBLISHED THESIS OR DISSERTATION

To cite an unpublished thesis or dissertation, give its author, title (in quotation marks), academic institution, and date.

> 34. Scott Riney, "The School of the Hills: American Indians and the Rapid City Indian School, 1889–1933" (Ph.D. diss., Arizona State University, 1996), 13.

ILLUSTRATION

In citing an illustration in a printed text, give both the page number on which the illustration appears and the figure or plate number, if one is provided.

35. William E. Taylor and Harriet G. Warkel, *A Shared Heritage: Art by Four African Americans* (Indianapolis: Indianapolis Museum of Art, 1996), 62, plate 39.

SOUND RECORDING

Notes for sound recordings, including audiotapes, compact disks, and records, begin with the composer's name, followed by the title of the recording (underlined or italicized), and the name of the performer. Also provide the name of the recording company and the number.

36. Gustav Holst, *The Planets*, Royal Philharmonic Orchestra, André Previn, Telarc compact disk 80133.

For an anonymous work or a collection of works by several composers, begin with the title.

37. *Virtuoso Recorder Music*, Amsterdam Loeki Stardust Quartet, Decca compact disk 414 277-2.

FILM OR VIDEOCASSETTE

A note for a film or videocassette should include the title of the film, the name of the producer and director, the playing time, the name of the production company, and the date. Videocassettes should be identified as such.

38. "Forever Free," *The Civil War*, prod. Ken Burns, 11 hours, PBS Video, 1990, videocassette.

INTERVIEW

A note for an interview that has been published or broadcast on radio or television should include the name of the person interviewed, the title of the interview (if any), the name of the person who conducted the interview, the medium in which the interview appeared (radio, television, book, journal), and the facts of publication.

39. H. Ross Perot, interview by Mike Wallace, *60 Minutes*, Columbia Broadcasting System, 8 March 1992.

PERSONAL COMMUNICATION

A note for an interview you have conducted in person or by telephone should include the name of the person you interviewed, the words "interview by author," the place of the interview, if applicable, and the date of the interview.

40. Hector LaForge, telephone interview by author, 4 April 1993.

A personal letter or memorandum to you should be cited in the same way as a personal interview.

> 41. Deena Swanson, letter to author, 22 August 1990.

REFERENCE WORK

In a note for a standard reference work that is arranged alphabetically, such as a dictionary or an encyclopedia, omit the publication information and the volume and page references. You must, however, note the edition if it is not the first. After the name and edition of the work, use the abbreviation "s.v." (for *sub verbo,* "under the word") followed by the title of the entry in quotation marks.

> 42. *Encyclopaedia Britannica,* 15th ed., s.v. "steam power."

> 43. *Merriam-Webster's Collegiate Dictionary,* 10th ed., s.v. "civilization."

BIBLICAL REFERENCE

When referring to a passage from the Bible, cite the book (abbreviated), chapter, and verse, either in the text or in a note. Do not provide a page number. In your first biblical reference, identify the version of the Bible you are using; in subsequent references, abbreviate the version.

> 44. Matt. 20.4–9 Revised Standard Version.

> 45. 1 Chron. 4.13–15 RSV.

Chapters and verses in biblical references have traditionally been separated by a colon, but in current usage they are separated by a period.

INDIRECT SOURCE

If material you wish to use from a source has been taken from another source, it is always preferable to find and consult the original source. If this is not possible, you must acknowledge both the original source of the material and your own source for the information.

> 46. George Harmon Knoles, *The Jazz Age Revisited: British Criticism of American Civilization during the 1920s* (Stanford: Stanford University Press, 1955), 31, quoted in C. Vann Woodward, *The Old World's New World* (Oxford: Oxford University Press, 1991), 46.

Electronic sources

WEB SITE

To cite a document that is available on the World Wide Web, the following information should be included: the author's name, if known; the title of the document, in quotation marks; the title of the complete work, if applicable, in italics or underlined; the date of the publication or last revision (if not known, use "n.d."); the URL, in angle brackets; and the date of access, in parentheses. The following models are based on the guidelines found in *Online! A Reference Guide to Using Internet Sources* by Andrew Harnack and Eugene Kleppinger (New York: St. Martin's Press, 1997).

> 47. Robert Brigham, "The Wars for Vietnam," n.d., <http://www.vassar.edu/vietnam/index.html> (30 October 1997).

GOPHER SITE

Include the author's name, if available; the title; the title of the complete work, if applicable; the version and date, if known; the gopher address; and the date of access.

> 48. "United States Note to the U.S.S.R., May 6, 1960," *United States Intelligence Flights over the Soviet Union: The U-2 Incident,* n.d., <gopher://wiretap.spies.com:70/00/Gov/US-History/u2> (4 November 1997).

FTP SITE

Include the author's name, if available; the title; the title of the complete work, if applicable; the version and date, if known; the ftp address; and the date of access.

> 49. Donna C. Prater, "Sabers and Soapsuds: Dragoon Women on the Frontier, 1833–1861," September 1992, <ftp://history.cc.ukans.edu/pub/history/general/articles/prater1.art> (12 November 1997).

E-MAIL MESSAGE

Include the author's name; the author's e-mail address; the subject line from the posting; the date of publication; the type of communication; and the date of access.

> 50. Lisa O'Donnell, <lodon@mnnf.k12.mn.us> "Re: Grave Sites," 10 November 1997, personal e-mail (11 November 1997).

LISTSERV OR NEWSGROUP MESSAGE

Include the author's name; the author's e-mail address; the subject line from the posting; the date of publication; the name of the listserv or newsgroup; and the date of access.

> 51. John Halberstam, <jhalberstam@tma.edu> "Lakota Diaspora after 1862," 11 December 1997, <H -ETHNIC@h-net.msu.edu> (12 December 1997).

SYNCHRONOUS COMMUNICATION

Include the speaker(s), if applicable; the title and date of the event, if appropriate; the type of communication; the source; the address; and the date of communication.

> 52. Lucian Saunier, personal communication, Diversity University MOO, telnet moo.du.org.8888 (11 November 1997).

Models for bibliography entries

Your bibliography provides a list of the books, articles, and other sources you used in preparing your paper. It must include all the works you cited in your notes; it may also include other works that you consulted but did not cite. However, avoid the temptation to pad your bibliography; list only materials you did in fact use.

You should list works in your bibliography alphabetically by authors' last names. If your bibliography is long, you may wish to divide it into sections. You might, for example, create separate headings such as "Primary Sources" and "Books and Articles." If you have used manuscripts or other unpublished sources, you might list these separately as well.

Books

A typical bibliography entry for a book contains the following information:

- The author's full name, last name first, followed by a period
- The full title of the book, underlined or italicized, followed by a period
- The city of publication, followed by a colon
- The name of the publisher, followed by a comma
- The date of publication, followed by a period

Typically, the first line of a bibliography entry is typed flush left, and subsequent lines are indented. Individual entries should be single-spaced; double-space between entries.

BASIC FORM FOR A BOOK

> Wheeler, Marjorie Spruill. *Votes for Women: The Woman Suffrage Movement in Tennessee, the South, and the Nation.* Knoxville: University of Tennessee Press, 1995.

TWO OR MORE AUTHORS

An entry for a book with two or more authors should begin with the name of the first author listed on the title page, last name first. The names of the other authors are given in normal order.

> Linden-Ward, Blanche, and Carol Hurd Green. *American Women in the 1960s: Changing the Future.* New York: Twayne, 1993.

> Appleby, Joyce, Lynn Hunt, and Margaret Jacob. *Telling the Truth about History.* New York: Norton, 1994.

NOTE: For books with more than three authors, you may use the first author's name followed by the Latin term "et al." ("and others") in place of the other authors' names (for example, "Doe, Jane, et al.").

AUTHOR'S NAME IN THE TITLE

Begin the bibliography entry with the author's name, even if it appears in the title.

> Stalin, Joseph. *Stalin's Letters to Molotov, 1925–1936.* Edited by Lars T. Lih, Oleg V. Naumov, and Oleg V. Khlevniuk. Translated by Catherine A. Fitzpatrick. New Haven: Yale University Press, 1995.

ANONYMOUS WORK

If the author of a work is unknown, list the work in the bibliography by its title. If the title begins with an article (*A, An,* or *The*), alphabetize the book according to the first letter of the next word.

> *Images of America: A Panorama of History in Photographs.* Washington, D.C.: Smithsonian Books, 1989.

EDITED OR COMPILED WORK WITHOUT AN AUTHOR

List a book by the last name of the editor, translator, or compiler if no author appears on the title page (as in a collection or anthology).

> Prakash, Gyan, ed. *After Colonialism: Imperial Histories and Postcolonial Displacements.* Princeton: Princeton University Press, 1995.

EDITED WORK WITH AN AUTHOR

For a book with an author as well as an editor, the editor's name follows the title.

> Kahlo, Frida. *The Letters of Frida Kahlo: Cartas Apasionadas.* Edited by Martha Zamora. San Francisco: Chronicle Books, 1995.

TRANSLATED WORK

A translator's name, like an editor's, is placed after the title when an author's name is given. If a source has an editor and a translator, both should be listed.

> Aguilar Camin, Hector, and Lorenzo Meyer. *In the Shadow of the Mexican Revolution: Contemporary Mexican History, 1910–1989.* Translated by Luis Alberto Fierro. Austin: University of Texas Press, 1993.

> Noiriel, Gerard. *The French Melting Pot: Immigration, Citizenship, and National Identity.* Edited by Charles Tilly. Translated by Geoffroy de Laforcade. Minneapolis: University of Minnesota Press, 1996.

MULTIVOLUME WORK

For a multivolume work, include the number of volumes in the bibliography entry.

> *Freedom: A Documentary History of Emancipation, 1861–1867.* 4 vols. New York: Cambridge University Press, 1993.

If you have used a single volume of a multivolume set, cite only that volume. You can do this in one of two ways: giving the name of the volume first or the name of the series first.

> *The Wartime Genesis of Free Labor: The Upper South.* Edited by Ira Berlin. Vol. 1 of *Freedom: A Documentary History of Emancipation, 1861–1867.* New York: Cambridge University Press, 1993.

or

> *Freedom: A Documentary History of Emancipation, 1861–1867.* Vol. 1, *The Wartime Genesis of Free Labor: The Upper South.* Edited by Ira Berlin. New York: Cambridge University Press, 1993.

If an individual volume in a multivolume work does not have its own title, specify the volume by number.

> *Cambridge History of American Foreign Relations.* Vol. 1. Cambridge: Cambridge University Press, 1993.

If the volume or collection of volumes has an author, the entry should begin with the author's name (last name first), followed by a period.

ARTICLE IN A COLLECTION OR ANTHOLOGY

List an article in a collection or anthology by the author of the article. You may include the pages on which the article begins and ends.

> Breines, Wini. "The 'Other' Fifties: Beats and Bad Girls." In *Not June Cleaver: Women and Gender in Post-War America, 1945–1960,* 380–410. Philadelphia: Temple University Press, 1994.

LETTER IN A PUBLISHED COLLECTION

If you cite only one letter from a collection, you may list it as an individual letter in your bibliography.

> Debs, Eugene V. Letter to John Reed, 21 September 1918. In *Gentle Rebel: Letters of Eugene V. Debs,* edited by J. Robert Constantine. Urbana: University of Illinois Press, 1994.

However, if you cite several letters from the same collection, list only the collection.

> Debs, Eugene V. *Gentle Rebel: Letters of Eugene V. Debs.* Edited by J. Robert Constantine. Urbana: University of Illinois Press, 1994.

EDITION OTHER THAN THE FIRST

If you are using any edition other than the first, include the edition number in your bibliography.

> *Farm to Factory: Women's Letters, 1830–1860.* Edited by Thomas Dublin. 2d ed. New York: Columbia University Press, 1993.

WORK IN A SERIES

A series is a set of publications on the same general subject that is supervised by an editor or group of editors. Begin the entry with the author and title of the individual work from the series. Also include the title and editor of the series.

> Hughes, Steven C. *Crime, Disorder, and the Risorgimento: The Politics of Policing in Bologna.* Cambridge Studies in Italian History and Culture, edited by Giorgio Chittolini, vol. 4. Cambridge: Cambridge University Press, 1994.

Periodicals

A typical bibliography entry for an article in a journal includes the following information:

- The author's full name, last name first, followed by a period
- The title of the article, in quotation marks and followed by a period
- The name of the journal, underlined or italicized
- The volume number, in arabic numerals
- The date, in parentheses, followed by a colon
- The pages on which the article begins and ends, followed by a period

ARTICLE IN A JOURNAL PAGINATED BY VOLUME

Most scholarly journals are paginated consecutively throughout the volume. When citing an article from such a journal, it is not mandatory that you give the issue number.

> Hanley, Sarah. "Social Sites of Political Practice in France: Lawsuits, Civil Rights, and the Separation of Powers in Domestic and State Government, 1500–1800." *American Historical Review* 102 (1997): 27–52.

ARTICLE IN A JOURNAL PAGINATED BY ISSUE

If a journal paginates each issue separately, you must provide the issue number.

> Inness, Sherrie A. "On the Road and in the Air: Gender and Technology in Girls' Automobile and Airplane Serials, 1909–1932." *Journal of Popular Culture* 30, no. 2 (1996): 47–61.

NOTE: If you wish to include the month of publication, put it before the year: (March 1986). If you include the month, you do not need the issue number.

ARTICLE IN A POPULAR MAGAZINE

It is not necessary to give the volume number or issue number for an article in a popular magazine. If you include page numbers, they are preceded by a comma, not by a colon.

> Engelhardt, Tom. "Fifty Years under a Cloud: The Uneasy Search for Our Atomic History." *Harper's,* January 1996, 71–76.

NEWSPAPER ARTICLE

If you consulted various articles from a particular newspaper, you don't have to list the articles separately in the bibliography. Instead, provide just the name of the paper and the range of dates of the issues you consulted.

> *Louisville Courier-Journal,* 14 October–20 October 1997.

BOOK REVIEW

List a book review by the reviewer's last name. If the author of the review is not named, begin with the title of the review or, if the review is untitled, with the words "Review of."

> Falk, Candace. Review of *Better Red: The Writing and Resistance of Tillie Olsen and Meridel Le Sueur,* by Constance Coiner. *American Historical Review* 102 (1997): 208–9.

> Review of *The Clash: A History of U.S.-Japan Relations,* by Walter LeFeber. *Publishers Weekly,* 21 July 1997, 193.

Public documents

The same information should be provided as for notes (see pp. 57–59). In a paper on United States history, you may omit "United States" or "U.S." as the country in which a document was issued if it is clear in context.

PRESIDENTIAL PAPERS

Entries for these papers often begin with and are alphabetized by the president's name.

> Eisenhower, Dwight D. *Public Papers of the Presidents of the United States: Dwight D. Eisenhower, 1953.* Washington, D.C.: GPO, 1960.

EXECUTIVE DEPARTMENT DOCUMENT

Entries for these documents begin with the issuing department's name.

> U.S. General Accounting Office. *Desert Shield and Desert Storm Reports and Testimonies, 1991–93.* Washington, D.C.: General Accounting Office, 1994.

> U.S. Department of State. *Belarus.* Background Notes Series, no. 10344.

TESTIMONY BEFORE A COMMITTEE

If you cite or consult a transcript of testimony before a committee, begin the entry with the name of the committee.

> House Committee on Veterans' Affairs. *Radiation Research in the VA Involving Human Subjects: Hearing before the Committee on Veterans' Affairs.* 103d Cong., 2d sess. Washington: GPO, 1994.

CONGRESSIONAL COMMITTEE PRINT

Entries for these research reports should include the print number or date.

> U.S. Congress. Senate Committee on Foreign Relations. *Russia on the Eve of the Presidential Election: A Staff Report to the Committee on Foreign Relations.* 104th Cong., 2d sess., 1996.

TREATY

Begin the entry with the name of the issuing agency.

> U.S. Department of State. "Jay Treaty," 19 November 1794. TIAS no. 105. *United States Treaties and Other International Agreements,* vol. 2.

(See p. 59 for information about the TIAS number.)

UNITED STATES CONSTITUTION

If you cite the Constitution in your paper, you do not need to include it in your bibliography.

Other sources

UNPUBLISHED THESIS OR DISSERTATION

List an unpublished thesis or dissertation by its author's last name.

Riney, Scott. "The School of the Hills: American Indians and the Rapid City Indian School, 1889–1933." Ph.D. diss., Arizona State University, 1996.

ILLUSTRATION

Taylor, William E., and Harriet G. Warkel. *A Shared Heritage: Art by Four African Americans.* Indianapolis: Indianapolis Museum of Art, 1996.

SOUND RECORDING

List a sound recording by the composer's last name or, for a collection or an anonymous work, by the title of the recording. Include the recording company and number if they are provided.

Holst, Gustav. *The Planets.* Royal Philharmonic Orchestra. André Previn. Telarc compact disk 80133.

Virtuoso Recorder Music. Amsterdam Loeki Stardust Quartet. Decca compact disk 414 277-2.

FILM OR VIDEOCASSETTE

After the film title, include the name of the producer and director, the playing time, the production company, the date, and the medium.

The Civil War. Produced by Ken Burns. 11 hours. PBS Video, 1990. 9 videocassettes.

INTERVIEW

List an interview under the name of the person interviewed and provide the date of the interview.

Perot, H. Ross. Interview by Mike Wallace. *60 Minutes.* Columbia Broadcasting System, 8 March 1992.

PERSONAL COMMUNICATION

Because your reader will not have access to personal interviews you conducted or letters you received, there is no need to list these sources of information in your bibliography.

REFERENCE WORKS AND THE BIBLE

Well-known reference works and the Bible are usually not included in bibliographies.

INDIRECT SOURCE

If material you have taken from one source originally appeared in another source and you have not consulted the original yourself, your bibliography entry should begin with the original source but must include your own source for the information. The page numbers from both sources should be included.

> Knoles, George Harmon. *The Jazz Age Revisited: British Criticism of American Civilization during the 1920s,* 31. Stanford: Stanford University Press, 1955. Quoted in C. Vann Woodward, *The Old World's New World* (Oxford: Oxford University Press, 1991), 46.

Electronic sources

WEB SITE

> Brigham, Robert. "The Wars for Vietnam." n.d. <http://www.vassar.edu/vietnam/index.html> (30 October 1997).

GOPHER SITE

> "United States Note to the U.S.S.R., May 6, 1960." *United States Intelligence Fights over the Soviet Union: The U-2 Incident.* n.d. <gopher://wiretap.spies.com: 70/00/Gov/US-History/u2> (4 November 1997).

FTP SITE

> Prater, Donna C. "Sabers and Soapsuds: Dragoon Women on Frontier, 1833–1861." September 1992. <ftp: //history.cc.ukans.edu/pub/history/general/articles /prater1.art> (12 November 1997).

E-MAIL MESSAGE

> O'Donnell, Lisa. <lodon@mnnf.k12.mn.us> "Re: Grave Sites." 10 November 1997. Personal e-mail (11 November 1997).

LISTSERV OR NEWSGROUP MESSAGE

> Halberstam, John. <jhalberstam@tma.edu> "Lakota Diaspora after 1862." 11 December 1997. <H-ETHNIC@h -net.msu.edu> (12 December 1997).

SYNCHRONOUS COMMUNICATION

> Saunier, Lucian. Personal communication. Diversity University MOO. telnet moo.du.org.8888 (11 November 1997).

SAMPLE BIBLIOGRAPHY

Bibliography

Primary Sources

Columbus, Christopher. The Journal of Christo-
        pher Columbus. Translated by Cecil Jane.
        New York: Clarkson N. Potter, 1960.

Dawson, Christopher, ed. Mission to Asia. 1955.
        Reprint, Toronto: University of Toronto
        Press, 1980.

Mandeville, John. The Travels of Sir John Man-
        deville. Translated by C. W. R. D. Mose-
        ley. Harmondsworth, England: Penguin,
        1983.

Polo, Marco. The Travels of Marco Polo. Edited
        and translated by Ronald Latham. Har-
        mondsworth, England: Penguin, 1958.

Books and Articles

Allen, John L. "Lands of Myth, Waters of Won-
        der: The Place of the Imagination in the
        History of Geographical Exploration." In
        Geographies of the Mind: Essays in Histor-
        ical Geosophy, edited by David Lowenthal
        and Martyn J. Bowden, 41-62. New York:
        Oxford University Press, 1976.

Campbell, Mary B. The Witness and the Other
        World: Exotic European Travel Writing,
        400-1600. Ithaca: Cornell University
        Press, 1988.

Howard, Donald R. "The World of Mandeville's
        Travels." Yearbook of English Studies 1
        (1971): 1-17.

Mignolo, Walter D. The Darker Side of the
        Renaissance: Literacy, Territoriality, and
        Colonization. Ann Arbor: University of
        Michigan Press, 1995.

Skelton, R. A., D. B. Quinn, and W. P. Cumming.
      The Discovery of North America. New York:
      American Heritage Press, 1972.

Watts, Pauline Moffitt. "Prophecy and Discov-
      ery: On the Spiritual Origins of Christo-
      pher Columbus's 'Enterprise of the
      Indies.'" American Historical Review 90
      (1985): 73–102.

Appendix A.
Writing Guides
of Interest to Historians

The following books offer helpful guidance on stylistic matters and other writing concerns. The guides to writing in history, in addition to offering general writing advice, discuss how historians work and cover typical assignments in history, stylistic conventions, the research process, and documentation.

General writing guides

Hacker, Diana. *A Pocket Style Manual.* 2d ed. Boston: Bedford Books, 1997.

Hacker, Diana. *Rules for Writers.* 3d ed. Boston: Bedford Books, 1996.

Strunk, William, Jr., and E. B. White. *The Elements of Style.* 3d ed. New York: Macmillan, 1979.

Turabian, Kate L. *A Manual for Writers of Term Papers, Theses, and Dissertations.* 5th ed. Revised and expanded by Bonnie Birtwistle Honigsblum. Chicago: University of Chicago Press, 1987.

University of Chicago Press. *The Chicago Manual of Style.* 14th ed. Chicago: University of Chicago Press, 1993.

Guides to writing in history

Benjamin, Jules R. *A Student's Guide to History.* 4th ed. Boston: Bedford Books, 1997.

Marius, Richard. *A Short Guide to Writing about History.* 2d ed. New York: HarperCollins, 1995.

Steffens, Henry J., and Mary Jane Dickerson. *Writer's Guide to History.* Lexington, Mass.: D. C. Heath, 1987.

Appendix B.
Library Resources
in History

by Barbara Fister, Gustavus Adolphus College

While doing research in history, you will need to collect evidence and find commentary that helps you interpret it. Your library and the Internet offer many tools that will help you track down primary and secondary sources and answer questions that arise as you learn more about your topic. This appendix suggests helpful indexes, references, periodicals, and sources of primary documents. It also offers a sampler of electronic sources available through the Internet. The materials listed here are not available at all libraries, but they give you an idea of the range of resources available. Remember, too, that librarians are an extremely helpful resource. They can direct you to useful materials throughout your research process.

Indexes and bibliographies

America: History and Life. Santa Barbara, Calif., and Oxford: ABC-Clio, 1964–.

> Covers publications of all kinds on U.S. and Canadian history and culture in a chronological/regional format, offering abstracts of the publications covered. Available in computerized format.

American Historical Association Guide to Historical Literature. 3d ed. New York: Oxford University Press, 1995.

> Offers 27,000 citations to important historical literature, arranged in forty-eight sections covering theory, international history, and regional history. An indispensable guide recently updated to include current trends in historical research.

Historical Abstracts. Santa Barbara, Calif., and Oxford: ABC-Clio, 1955–.

> Covers world history (excluding the United States and Canada) from 1450. Available in computerized format.

Where to find overviews of topics in history

Black Women in America: An Historical Encyclopedia. Brooklyn: Carlson, 1993.

> A compilation of biographical and topical articles that constitutes a definitive history of African American women.

Civilizations of the Ancient Mediterranean. New York: Scribner's, 1988.

> Provides in-depth articles on life and culture in ancient Greece and Rome, including topics such as "Women in Rome" and "Myths and Cosmologies."

Civilizations of the Ancient Near East. New York: Scribner's, 1995.

> Provides surveys of the culture and history of Egypt, Syro-Palestine, Mesopotamia, and Anatolia.

Dictionary of American History. Rev. ed. New York: Scribner's, 1976.

> An encyclopedia of terms, places, and concepts in U.S. history. Similar sets include *Encyclopedia of the Confederacy* and *Encyclopedia of North American Colonies.* For biographical information, consult the *Dictionary of American Biography.*

Dictionary of Concepts in History. New York: Greenwood, 1986.

> Includes essays that define historiographic concepts and describe how the concepts were formed. Contains excellent bibliographies.

Dictionary of the Middle Ages. New York: Scribner's, 1982–89.

> The single most complete source covering people, events, ideas, movements, texts, and cultural features of the medieval world.

Encyclopedia of African-American Culture and History. New York: Macmillan Library Reference, 1996.

> A wide-ranging encyclopedia covering people, places, events, concepts, and topics.

Encyclopedia of American Social History. New York: Scribner's, 1993.

Covers topics such as religion, race, class, gender, popular culture, regionalism, and everyday life from pre-Columbian to modern times.

Encyclopedia of Asian History. New York: Scribner's, 1988.

Includes detailed articles on people, places, and events in Asian history. Covers Central Asia, South Asia, and the Far East.

Encyclopedia of Latin American History and Culture. New York: Scribner's, 1996.

Covers a wide variety of topics in more than five thousand articles that together constitute an overview of current knowledge about the region.

Encyclopedia of the Holocaust. New York: Macmillan, 1990.

Multivolume set that covers topics related to the Holocaust.

Encyclopedia of the United States in the Twentieth Century. New York: Scribner's, 1996.

An ambitious survey of American cultural, social, and intellectual history; organized as broad articles arranged by topic.

New Cambridge Modern History. Cambridge: Cambridge University Press, 1957–79.

Multivolume work covering 1493–1945 in chronological and topic order, giving detailed and lengthy narrative surveys of the times. Similar works by Cambridge University Press include those on ancient history, medieval history, and histories of regions and countries, such as the *Cambridge History of Africa.*

Oxford Encyclopedia of the Reformation. New York: Oxford University Press, 1996.

Multivolume set that covers people, places, events, documents, and ideas relevant to the Reformation.

Where to find concise information

SPECIALIZED DICTIONARIES

This list is just a sampling of dictionaries that survey important people, events, and topics for a variety of historical subjects.

The ABC-Clio Companion to Women's Progress in America.
    Santa Barbara, Calif.: ABC-Clio, 1994.

The Blackwell Companion to the Enlightenment. Oxford:
    Blackwell, 1991.

Critical Dictionary of the French Revolution. Cambridge: Har-
    vard University Press, 1989.

Dictionary of Afro-American Slavery. New York: Greenwood,
    1985.

Dictionary of the Russian Revolution. New York: Greenwood,
    1989.

Dictionary of Scandinavian History. New York: Greenwood,
    1986.

Dictionary of the Vietnam War. New York: Greenwood, 1988.

Historical Dictionary of the New Deal. New York: Greenwood,
    1985.

Historical Dictionary of the Progressive Era. New York:
    Greenwood, 1988.

Consult a librarian to see if there is a specialized dictionary
for your topic.

OTHER SOURCES

The Times Atlas of World History. Maplewood, N.J.: Ham-
    mond, 1993.

> Covers the world's past geographically. Other historical
> atlases include *The Historical and Cultural Atlas of African
> Americans, Historical Atlas of Britain,* and *Historical Atlas of
> Political Parties in the United States Congress, 1789–1989.*

The Timetables of History. New York: Simon and Schuster,
    1991.

> Covers politics, religion, the arts, science and technology,
> and daily life year by year, from ancient times to the pres-
> ent. Provides an interesting way to connect events occur-
> ring in different places and fields. Similar works: *A Chronol-
> ogy of the History of Science, 1450–1900; A Chronology of
> Irish History since 1500;* and *A World in Turmoil: An Inte-
> grated Chronology of the Holocaust and World War II.*

Where to find primary sources

There are many ways to find primary sources for historical
research. You can search your library catalog using the
names of historical figures as authors; you can also consult
anthologies of documents covering particular themes or peri-

ods in history. The following special materials can help you
find useful primary sources.

THE PRESS

American Periodicals Series, 1741–1900.

> Microfilm collection covering periodicals from the colonial
> period to the turn of the twentieth century.

Herstory.

> Microfilm collection covering alternative feminist periodicals
> published between 1960 and 1980. Offers an interesting
> documentary history of the women's movement.

The New York Times.

> The *Times* has been called "the newspaper of record" for its
> coverage of key events. Many libraries have it on microfilm
> going back to the first issue in 1851. An index to the *Times*
> itself constitutes a detailed chronology of events.

Readers' Guide to Periodical Literature.

> Index to popular magazines beginning in 1900; an earlier
> index, *Poole's Index to Periodical Literature,* covers
> 1802–1906.

The Times of London.

> This newspaper is available on microfilm at some libraries.
> An index covers 1785 to the present.

DIARIES, PAMPHLETS, AND BOOKS

The American Culture Series.

> A microfilm set, including a subject index, featuring books
> and pamphlets published between 1493 and 1875.

American Women's Diaries.

> A set of microfilmed diaries kept by women from New En-
> gland and the southern and western United States.

*Early English Books, 1475-1640; Early English Books,
1641–1700.*

> Offer a vast collection of early books on microfilm, with
> indexes.

PUBLIC DOCUMENTS

Many libraries house collections of state, federal, and United
Nations documents. These papers—which include committee
reports, agency records, and transcripts of hearings and

speeches — provide a particularly detailed record of public life. If your library does not have a documents collection, you might be able to borrow documents from a regional government documents depository. The following are some useful series.

Congressional Record. Washington, D.C.: GPO, 1874–.

> Covers debates and proceedings of Congress. Earlier series were called *Debates and Proceedings in the Congress of the United States* and *The Congressional Globe.* Similar records exist for other countries; for example, proceedings of the English Parliament can be found in *Hansard's Parliamentary Debates.*

Foreign Relations of the United States. Washington, D.C.: GPO, 1861–.

> Collection of documents, including diplomatic papers, correspondence, and memoranda, that provides a detailed record of U.S. foreign policy.

Public Papers of the Presidents of the United States. Washington, D.C.: GPO, 1909–.

> Includes major documents issued by the executive branch from Hoover's administration to the present. Many sets of papers from earlier presidencies have been published as well.

U.S. Serial Set. Washington, D.C.: GPO, 1789–1969.

> A vast compilation of a multitude of congressional documents. Some libraries have this set in microfiche.

LOCAL HISTORY COLLECTIONS

State and county historical societies often house a wealth of historical documents. Consider using their resources; you may find yourself working with material that no one has analyzed before.

Internet resources

The Internet is a medium of increasing importance for research. Internet discussion lists give historians a means of engaging in wide-ranging e-mail conversations about such focused topics as women's history, ethnic history, and African history. You can post questions, raise issues, or simply eavesdrop (called "lurking" in Internet jargon) as historians communicate informally. Electronic journals are a more formal means of communication through the Internet. Some electronic journals, such as the *Bryn Mawr Classical Review,* exist only in electronic format. Your library may also subscribe to electronic versions of print journals, making them available from any computer connected to the Internet.

The Internet is also an increasingly useful place to find primary sources. You can view photographs and drawings, play audio recordings of speeches or Supreme Court arguments, or find historical documents that you can print or save to your own computer.

As you use the Internet for research, make sure you assess the value of the material you find (see p. 9) and document where you found it (see pp. 62–63 and 71).

The Web sites listed here indicate some of the history resources available.

American Memory: Historical Collection from the National Digital Library Program. <http://lcweb2.loc.gov /ammem/ammemhome.html>

A site featuring digitized primary source materials from the Library of Congress, among them African American pamphlets, Civil War photographs, documents from the Continental Congress and the Constitutional Convention of 1774–90, materials on woman suffrage, and oral histories.

Euro-docs: Primary Historical Documents from Western Europe — Selected Transcriptions, Facsimiles, and Translations. <http://www.lib.byu.edu/~rdh/eurodocs/>

A collection of primary sources organized by country and period.

Gateway to World History. <http://www.hartford-hwp.com /gateway/index.html>

A site providing resources for the study and teaching of world history, including archives of historical documents, information on courses and departments, and professional resources for historians.

Historical Text Archive. <http://www.msstate.edu/Archives /History>

Easy access through well-organized links to the oldest and largest Internet site for historical documents. Emphasis is on U.S. history, but coverage of other parts of the world is growing.

Index of Resources for Historians. <http://kuhttp.cc.ukans .edu/history/index.html>

A vast list of more than 1,700 links to sites of interest to historians, arranged alphabetically by general topic. Some links are to general-reference sources, but many are on historical topics. A good place to start an exploration of the Internet sources for history.

Internet Medieval Sourcebook. <http://www.fordham.edu /halsall/sbook.html>

A huge collection of Internet-accessible primary texts, well organized by topic and period. There is a *Modern History Sourcebook* offering texts relating to modern Western history from the Reformation to the present at <http://www.fordham.edu/halsall/mod/modsbook.html>.

SITES FOR GENERAL RESEARCH PURPOSES

Search engines are programs that locate Internet sources containing the search terms you type in. Because they don't screen for quality and seek matches based exclusively on the words you type, they often produce vast numbers of irrelevant or useless results. They work best when you have a fairly specific topic. "Meta search engines" run search terms through several search engines at once.

Metacrawler. <http://www.metacrawler.com>

Sends your search to a number of different search engine programs at once and quickly returns your results. For best results, place a search phrase in quotation marks.

Internet directories list Internet sites organized in some fashion, usually by subject. Sometimes a good directory will lead you to information more quickly than a search engine, especially if your topic is fairly broad.

The Argus Clearinghouse. <http://www.clearinghouse .net>

A source of guides to resources across the disciplines, with an emphasis on scholarly uses of Internet materials.

Some Web sites are designed to help you discover and use special kinds of Internet resources. The following two sites listed can put you in touch with electronic discussions and electronic library catalogs.

Directory of Scholarly and Professional E-Conferences. <http://n2h2.com/KOVACS/>

This site lists and describes discussion groups of various types — e-mail discussion groups, newsgroups, and interactive MOOs and MUDs, programs that create spaces on the network in which participants can move around and manipulate objects, all through typed messages transmitted to participants simultaneously. Emphasis is on discussion groups that are academic or professional.

Webcats: Library Catalogues on the World Wide Web.
   <http://library.usask.ca/hywebcat/>

An international directory of online library catalogs available through the Web. Geographical organization makes it easy to find a library of interest.